Legal Data and Information in Practice

Legal Data and Information in Practice provides readers with an understanding of how to facilitate the acquisition, management, and use of legal data in organizations such as libraries, courts, governments, universities, and start-ups.

Presenting a synthesis of information about legal data that will furnish readers with a thorough understanding of the topic, the book also explains why it is becoming crucial that data analysis be integrated into decision-making in the legal space. Legal organizations are looking at how to develop data-driven insights for a variety of purposes and it is, as Sutherland shows, vital that they have the necessary skills to facilitate this work. This book will assist in this endeavour by providing an international perspective on the issues affecting access to legal data and clearly describing methods of obtaining and evaluating it. Sutherland also incorporates advice about how to critically approach data analysis.

Legal Data and Information in Practice will be essential reading for those in the law library community who are based in English-speaking countries with a common law tradition. The book will also be useful to those with a general interest in legal data, including students, academics engaged in the study of information science and law.

Sarah A. Sutherland is President and CEO at the Canadian Legal Information Institute (CanLII) where she works on advancing CanLII's strategic priorities of providing access to law. She writes and presents regularly on legal data internationally and has a bi-monthly column on Slaw.ca.

Legal Data and Information in Practice

How Data and the Law Interact

Sarah A. Sutherland

Routledge
Taylor & Francis Group

LONDON AND NEW YORK

Cover image: Photo by CHUTTERSNAP on Unsplash

First published 2022
by Routledge
2 Park Square, Milton Park, Abingdon, Oxon OX14 4RN

and by Routledge
605 Third Avenue, New York, NY 10158

Routledge is an imprint of the Taylor & Francis Group, an informa business

© 2022 Sarah A. Sutherland

British Library Cataloguing-in-Publication Data
A catalogue record for this book is available from the British Library

Library of Congress Cataloging-in-Publication Data
Names: Sutherland, Sarah A., author.
Title: Legal data and information in practice : how data and the law interact / Sarah A. Sutherland.
Description: Abingdon, Oxon ; New York, NY : Routledge, 2022. | Includes bibliographical references and index.
Identifiers: LCCN 2021040617 (print) | LCCN 2021040618 (ebook) | ISBN 9780367649906 (hardback) | ISBN 9780367649883 (paperback) | ISBN 9781003127307 (ebook)
Subjects: LCSH: Law--English-speaking countries--Information services. | Legal research--English-speaking countries--Data processing. | Electronic information resource searching--English-speaking countries.
Classification: LCC K87 .S88 2022 (print) | LCC K87 (ebook) | DDC 343.09/99--dc23/eng/20211005
LC record available at https://lccn.loc.gov/2021040617
LC ebook record available at https://lccn.loc.gov/2021040618

ISBN: 978-0-367-64990-6 (hbk)
ISBN: 978-0-367-64988-3 (pbk)
ISBN: 978-1-003-12730-7 (ebk)

DOI: 10.4324/9781003127307

Typeset in Sabon
by Taylor & Francis Books

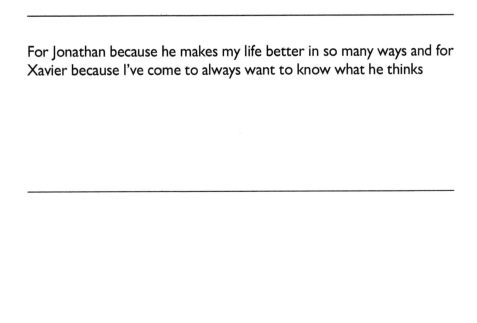

For Jonathan because he makes my life better in so many ways and for Xavier because I've come to always want to know what he thinks

Contents

Illustrations

Figures

Tables

Acknowledgements

There are so many people to thank who provided so much help and insight in the writing of this book. First I would like to thank my partner Jonathan Cross, without whom life would not have passed with as much joy. He has been so supportive throughout this process and through my life.

I would also like to thank my colleagues at CanLII and Lexum who have shared their insights and knowledge with me as I have learned and written about this topic. I want especially to thank Xavier Beauchamp-Tremblay who has had so many discussions with me over the last six years on this and many other topics, and who graciously gave me feedback and shared his thoughts through this process. Alisa Lazear, Ivan Mokanov, Marc-André Morrisette, and Frédéric Pelletier also were great help with sharing their insights and talking things through with me as I learned.

Many people graciously spoke with me about legal data around the world and in different contexts, without whom this book would have been significantly diminished: Kim Nayyer, Kristin Hodgins, Shannon Salter, Ed Walters, Pablo Arredondo, Mariya Badeva-Bright, Jules Winterton, Daniel Hoadley, Sara Frug, Jerrold Soh, Philip Chung, Andrew Mobray, Jason Morris, Carina Pillay, Michael Lissner, V.C. Vivekanandan, and Neil de Toit. Thank you all.

I am grateful to Guy Robertson for mentoring me through the process of bringing my first book into the world, from encouraging me to write a book proposal to giving me feedback on my draft. Finally, I would like to thank my friend Analise Hoffman who was so wonderfully supportive and insightful through this process.

Heidi Lowther and Elizabeth Risch at Routledge have been very helpful through this process and I am grateful for their advice and guidance as I worked through this process for the first time.

Introduction

Recent years have seen the accelerated adoption of technological innovations in the legal sector driven by advances in computing. This includes developments such as the growing use of computer applications in legal practice and increased focus on quantitative methods in legal scholarship. These changes have mainly been driven by technological improvements in applications like natural language processing, which have made it possible to approach the law in new ways. Researchers are exploring new ways of understanding the law, and the legal industry is looking for ways to change current business models and better serve social needs. These changes will have significant implications for legal systems around the world and for the people who are governed by them of one kind or another.

These innovations are driven by data, notably data about the law, the legal system, and legal businesses, and without access to substantial quantities of that data, they will not be able to be deployed to their full potential. That said, accessing this data is frequently problematic, with issues like privacy concerns limiting access. There also have to be changes in work processes and systems to ensure that the required data is collected. Even where data is available for use it may not be suitable for desired applications.

This book will discuss some of the particular aspects of data in the legal sector and how it can be understood, accessed, and used, to facilitate these changes and create new opportunities into the future. It is aimed at those who do the work of developing, providing access to, managing, and using legal data including information professionals, people working in courts and parliamentary bodies, publishers, developers, researchers, and legal professionals. Learning more about this topic will ensure that needed resources are established and the particular advantages and limitations of the law as a data source are understood as systems are built and projects planned.

These technological developments are happening at the same time as cultural and legal forces are changing expectations for how the law will be practiced, developed, and studied. We have increased expectations that technological change will happen quickly, and that systems will experience efficiency gains. Actors in many legal systems around the world are making changes to how public data associated with the law is made available, and they are anticipating these changes where that is not happening yet. Technologies associated with analysis of the substantial sizes of documents associated with legal materials have also advanced to the point where advances can be made with more ease than was previously possible.

In tandem with the pressures and possibilities associated with increased use of technological tools in law, there are powerful forces pushing for stasis. Legal systems can be ponderous to change, but this has real advantages. We need societies with relatively constant rules that allow us to live our lives with confidence knowing what is allowed and prohibited. Without this, we would be vulnerable to capricious governments that could change rules around us and leave us exposed to unjust repercussions. That said, there are certainly many new opportunities opening up to explore ways to make the law and the way it interacts with society better and more efficient.

One of the reasons the law has been so recalcitrant to productivity gains is because of the need for human inputs. The law has traditionally been a highly paid profession, and people working in the industry have had the social and economic power to maintain this over time. There are many opportunities for increased productivity through improved processes and other interventions, but the main source of this change is finding ways to use less human intervention for the same amount of work.

The desire to find these gains is understandable: it opens the possibility to increase the profitability of the sector while decreasing the costs associated with the administration of justice. However, planning to increase efficiencies by removing human input from the systems that govern us has the potential to have significant negative effects. As with any change to the legal system, these changes must be watched closely. Computational systems that work in the field of law will need to do the same. I would like to invite a critical approach to developing these tools and what is required to do that well and an openness to looking at human needs and aptitudes before assuming that artificial intelligence or other applications are superior.

The law is a special field for several reasons. Firstly, it is integral to people's lives, both in that what the laws are and how they are enforced can result in outcomes that range from deciding whether people can live with their children, if businesses will succeed or fail, or if people will be imprisoned or even executed. The importance of the decisions made in peoples affairs is reflected in the detail about their lives that is included in the documents that comprise much court data in particular. While in most cases legal proceedings are public, the balance of how accessible the data should be is something that each legal system needs to navigate, and the bodies like courts that issue documents should take responsibility for deciding what the appropriate balance should be.

"Scientific practice is grounded on a commitment to sharing data and enabling others to replicate findings. But the law's conception of openness is different, a commitment to carrying out public acts in a public space. A scientist might restrict access to a lab and still claim that the research she conducts there is "open." Closed proceedings in a legal setting, on the other hand, are only tolerated in extraordinary circumstances." (Pah et al. 2020, 135)

The law carries the full weight of the state in how it can implement the will of parliamentary bodies, courts, and tribunals. This creates incentives for people to pay for as much legal representation as they are able to: "in societies like ours the command of the public force is entrusted to judges in certain cases, and the whole powers of the state will be put forth, if necessary, to carry out their judgments and decrees" (Holmes, 1897). The inequality of ability to pay means that some people effectively have different rules applied to them than others do.

Though there is room in the current system for some addition of capacity, it is unlikely to be enough to alleviate the need for access to justice. There are significant gaps in access to professional legal assistance around the world, and technological solutions are one way to bridge them. Approximately 80% of people with legal problems internationally do not get help from a lawyer, and it is not possible to expand the current system to include four times the number of clients currently being served without significant changes (Walters 2021). That said, there is significant room for development of technical applications that will improve the ways societies function and the ways the legal industry works.

These technological advances will require access to extensive data. Some of the main avenues for development involve machine learning, which is anticipated to help automate tasks like simple decision making and certain processes. This approach requires large amounts of data, and has concerns associated with it that cannot be overlooked. These include both technical and cultural issues. Looking ahead brings more considerations. The shift toward use of machine learning and other technologies in the practice of law is the result of long term developments in technology adoption. The work being implemented now is years away from the primary research that showed initial proof of concept, and there continues to be work being done that expands the potential for what can be developed in the future.

However, there are real opportunities to improve the operations of legal organizations now by integrating data driven business practices: "Using the unique data stored in their [law firms'] systems, legal service organizations could differentiate themselves in ways other than price that clients will value" (Grady 2018, 15). The introduction of integration of concepts like probability with empirical data to back up the analysis is a promising way to better understand outcomes and serve clients.

This kind of development has the advantage of not requiring significant development to implement, because the technology and concepts are well understood, so there will be less risk in implementing it. This is important because one of the most important elements of technological innovation in law is robustness: systems need to be resilient at a system and not just a component level. In order to be successful any system will need to be dependable (Chatila 2020).

Outside the application of known concepts to research and business operations I am less enthusiastic about the potential for data-based research and applications to create substantial change in the world's legal systems in the near term. There are gaps and barriers to overcome, and it is unlikely that many of the developments futurists anticipate will ever come to pass, or that we would want them to if they are in fact possibilities.

Many of these initiatives will require extensive reorganization of the processes that create the required data, and this would represent a significant shift in priorities for how the law is administered. Laws are the agreed upon norms that human societies adopt, and they should address the needs of those societies. It would be appropriate to decide that the fact that they are conducive for use in particular technical applications should be irrelevant unless the technical applications will also serve the needs of those societies. Human needs should come first.

How to use this book

My goal in writing this book is to do what I can to help share the tools people can use to improve the legal system using the data that is already around us and give some insight into what is possible for the future. I believe data driven methodologies have the potential to do many things:

- To create research tools that give better answers to people's questions
- To decrease the cost of legal services
- To open new areas of research for academics and students to explore
- To improve the profitability of legal practice
- To provide better understanding of the legal system and where it succeeds and where it fails
- To help us better to understand what a fair system would look like

Improved understanding, collection, interpretation, and application of data has the potential to make those things possible. We can take the learnings and technologies developed in other fields and turn them toward the legal space to start working toward these goals, but we need to understand what we are looking at first. I do not claim to have all the answers, but with this book I hope to give you the tools to make the system better.

It is not possible in a book of this size to discuss the situation for all aspects of this subject around the world. I have focused on English speaking countries with common law traditions, but the technical aspects of analysis and how it can be applied are transferrable to other contexts. I have spoken with people internationally to try to get a cosmopolitan perspective, but there will be parts of the book that do not speak directly to a particular circumstance and where the terms of art used are different from what may be used locally — for this I ask your indulgence. My intention is to give a starting point for readers to understand the issues and move forward from rather than create an exhaustive resource that outlines every local practice or circumstance.

My goal is to provide a grounding in the subject, so that people with a technical background can understand the particular issues and concerns related to data in the legal sector and people with a legal background can understand how to approach understanding data and how it can be used. I hope that by meeting in the middle these two groups can create to explore the potential benefits the use of data in law can bring.

Book overview

The first chapter explains the benefits to using data to better understand processes and to support decision making in law. These approaches are widely used in other disciplines and industries but have been less used in law. Improvements in the availability of suitable technologies and data make it easier to bring these techniques into research and management of legal organizations to make more evidence-based decisions. There are many kinds of legal organizations, which all have different priorities and needs. These include challenges and opportunities, potential sources of data, limitations of existing systems, and some ways data is currently being used. There are many different issues affecting legal data around the world, including privacy laws, legacy investment in systems, legal publishing norms, legal regulation, and culture. This will give some additional information about how legal data is approached internationally.

The second chapter discusses how there are many possible sources for legal data. Some are openly available, while some are available by subscription, and some are internal to organizations. Each of these can convey different information, and sometimes they can be combined to give more specific insights. Governments around the world have been making more data available in recent years. Some of this is in the form of open data, which researchers can use with limited restrictions, and some has more limitations. The availability of primary law for use as data is particularly uneven around the world. Business processes are some of the most valuable sources of data used in business. As these systems are more widely available and adopted, this will be a new source of value generation. This data can supplement business process and government data to allow for further understanding of the legal system.

The third chapter explains that there are several different types of data that can be used for analysis. At a high level, these include numerical, categorical, and free text data. The most commonly available type of data in law is free text. Various techniques can be used to make it more computationally tractable, including extracting numerical and categorical data programmatically. Free text data can also be used as a source for tools that analyze language itself. They can also be used as feeds for other textual analysis techniques including several artificial intelligence applications such as self learning. There are many possible file formats used to deliver legal data. These include tagged formats like CSV, JSON, and XML, and document first formats like PDF or DOCX. Each of these can support different uses with advantages and limitations.

The fourth chapter discusses multiple ways to approach data analysis. Each of these is appropriate for different kinds of data and to convey different insights. Statistical techniques can be used to analyze legal data to draw conclusions: they can be used to show that datasets are demonstrating different outcomes for particular sets of participants, or if they are likely to reflect natural variation. As machine learning tools become more readily available and easier to use, text mining is more accessible for people who want to understand legal data better. People are using machine learning and other applications to build tools to assist with tasks like composition, classification, and developing commentary. Many applications are easier to use than others, with some becoming very accessible, while others are still several years away from commercial development.

The fifth chapter discusses how to interpret legal data. Analysis of data requires critical thinking about how to approach problems, such as what kinds of problems can be solved with better information. Information can be valuable for many reasons: it may illuminate an issue that is not clear or be valuable to understand a situation better. It may also facilitate making better decisions, but available data may be insufficient to drive decision making. In these cases, it can be necessary to analyze what is available, and what additional data could be collected that would fill in gaps. When deciding what data to collect, it is important to evaluate how useful it will be, and what it can or cannot say. This gives rise to important issues around validity of findings and the use of measures to assess progress on an ongoing basis when individuals' performance is evaluated on data that is not directly related to outcomes. It can be as important to know when to stop collecting data as it is to know how to find and interpret it, as it is often necessary to make decisions based on imperfect data.

The sixth chapter deals with issues specific to legal data. Legal data was often not created with the intention that it would be used as data at all. Instead, it is usually the result of events the creators understood to be distinct to a particular set of facts, such as a court case. This can make it difficult to analyze it in the ways other data more systematic data is analyzed. The most common criterion used for recording data about particular events in law is that they are unusual, because legal systems frequently focus on defining ranges of possible outcomes. Common outcomes are not considered to be as interesting. This is true of data from courts' handling of cases, client files in law firms, and the way legislators define potential outcomes in legislation. Statistical analysis usually focusses on defining the most common results and variability. This means that when many data points are missing or not recorded as in most legal contexts, traditional statistical analysis cannot give reliable results.

The seventh chapter gives an overview of the issues surrounding artificial intelligence in law. There is a great deal of hype on this topic, and while there is room for optimism, there are also concerns that data is being used inappropriately and stronger claims are being made than are warranted. We need to be sophisticated in accepting claims about what is possible. Many companies have started making artificial intelligence powered applications to assist in different kinds of tasks, and there are concerns that there is insufficient data in legal systems to be used to run many of these tools reliably. So far, these applications have been primarily sold to professional users. While there is hope that artificial intelligence will help to democratize legal advice and ameliorate problems like backlogs in courts, there have been technical and regulatory limits that have restricted many of them. It will be interesting to see how this field matures in coming years.

The eight chapter discusses the law and politics of legal data. Legal systems have differences that affect what legal data is available for use, because levels of investment in infrastructure and the legal status of law vary greatly. In some places which have made extensive investment in open data, statistical information about topics like court processes and the criminal system is starting to be made available. In common law countries court proceedings have been accessible to the public in the absence of compelling reasons to the contrary. However, as more case law is available online, privacy concerns have been raised. How this is handled varies greatly by jurisdiction. There are many different levels of investment and control over how accessible legal data is, and considerable variation in cultural expectations of how legal data is treated affect what is available.

The ninth chapter discusses how the future is likely to unfold for legal data. The law has lagged other areas of research and industry in the adoption of data-based research and decision making, but this does not have to continue, and there are increasing pressures to make sure it does not. Many people are pushing governments to provide more data-based laws: at a simple level this includes publishing legal documents in computer readable formats that can be more easily integrated into applications. These are relatively simple improvements, but they have the potential to improve access and accessibility in many places. Using legal data to drive better understanding and decision making opens opportunities for the future, but there are legitimate concerns. Nevertheless, there is still significant room for data driven innovation in the legal space, especially if it is considered, and we are careful to avoid negative consequences for individuals and communities.

Conclusion

Some of the most public calls for technologically driven reform of the legal system come from people who may not understand it well, and I would have more confidence if they spent the time to understand the underlying structure of the law and why things are done the way they are before calling for them to be changed. One of the main sources of hope for progress is in the area of artificial intelligence driven applications that can help people with routine issues and tasks, but there is currently faster growth in the development if these systems than there is development of capacity to consume and use the results to build value in a sophisticated way. This situation creates significant opportunities for people who are open to developing the expertise to take on leadership roles in this area. One of the reasons I wanted to write this book is to help readers learn more about it. I hope it will be a jumping off point for you to integrate these tools into your work and research.

References

Chatila, Raja. 2020. "Can AI Systems Be Trustworthy?" Presented at the JURIX 2020: 33rd International Conference on Legal Knowledge and Information Systems, Virtual, December 11.

Grady, Kenneth A. 2018. "Mining Legal Data: Collecting and Analyzing 21st Century Gold." In *Data-Driven Law: Data Analytics and the New Legal Services*, edited by Edward Walters, 11–32. Boca Raton, FL: Auerbach Publications.

Holmes, Jr., Oliver Wendell. 1897. "The Path of the Law." *Harvard Law Review* 10: 457.

Walters, Ed. 2021. (CEO at Fastcase), in discussion with the author.

Chapter 1

Legal data overview

1.1 Introduction

This book will demonstrate that there is great potential for better availability, understanding, and use of data about the law itself and about legal institutions, which can be used to improve understanding and processes within the sector. Sources of this data are varied and include data created as part of processes within legal organizations, the documents that make up the law itself, and experimental data generated to explore legal aspects of human societies. This data, used creatively and carefully, can help accomplish many things, such as:

- Improving the profitability of a legal practice
- Delivering insights into the way decisions are made
- Conveying understanding of how the legal system affects different segments of society
- Developing computer applications that create value

There are significant benefits to using data to better understand processes and to support decision making. This is widely practiced in other disciplines and industries. Until recently this has been less the case in law, but this is starting to change. Improvements in the availability of suitable technologies and data make it easier to use these techniques to make more evidence-based decisions and gain insights into how law affects society and how to improve methodologies.

Data is not a panacea, but there is a great deal of room to improve things in law. The introduction of artificial intelligence will not end war or resolve all contract disputes, but ending a given percentage of unnecessary disputes is within reach (Walker 2019, 13). Laws define the rules that human beings use to navigate complex relationships at societal levels, and these relationships will always contain complexities that require the creativity and insight humans possess. In the immediate term however, focusing on incremental improvements can bring considerable benefits, and in time the full potential of data driven methodologies will become clear.

DOI: 10.4324/9781003127307-1

1.2 Why look at data?

One of the great stories of the last 250 years has been the increase in productivity in many industries and the accompanying improvements in living conditions for a large proportion of the world's population. However, these productivity gains have not been consistent across sectors, with fields like medicine, education, and law, which require extensive human inputs that cannot be automated, lagging. This has been followed in recent years by a narrative about how artificial intelligence will change the ways people work and live, and that knowledge workers, like lawyers, will have their jobs disrupted in the near future in the same way manufacturing workers have had their jobs disrupted in the last twenty to thirty years.

How this will happen, or whether it will happen at all, remains to be seen, but it is clear that these changes will rely on data to develop the proposed systems, and they will not be possible without it. All the applications being proposed and launched that are described as being based on artificial intelligence or algorithms could just as correctly be described as being based on data. Many of these systems are anticipated to run on machine learning. These are sophisticated applications which use extensive data to draw conclusions on different situations which are anticipated to follow the same patterns. How to get this data and how to know whether it is predictive of expected patterns in other situations is less certain.

Prior generations of artificial intelligence development in the 1980s were usually based on hard coding behaviors into system, so that direct decisions could be made about how they would react in particular situations. This approach had issues with scale, because it could not use additional computing power without significant additional human input. In contrast, artificial intelligence applications now primarily use machine learning and complex statistical analyses based on ingesting enormous amounts of existing data, and the systems create the complexity needed primarily through computing power with considerably less human input. This is one of the shifts that makes artificial intelligence now seem more transformative than it did then. The ability to scale these applications creates the promise that artificial intelligence can deliver efficiency gains in knowledge-based work where in the past it could not achieve the required complexity.

In his book *On Legal AI*, Joshua Walker describes a "Cambrian explosion" of legal innovation happening now, but he argues that much of the publicity surrounding it is "marketing pablum" to fool demanding clients, and it is not based in substantial value or technical developments that warrant the hype (Walker 2019, 26). Whether his pessimism is warranted remains to be seen, but "artificial intelligence" is at least as much a marketing as a technical term. That said, better quality data that is used in mathematically justified ways can significantly improve the quality of the resulting applications. Being sophisticated about what particular datasets can support makes clients better able to select products effectively. This is important because there are real needs for improvements in legal systems around the world, and contrary to the alarmist rhetoric some have used to discuss these changes, there is room for many stakeholders to benefit.

There are substantial unmet needs for legal services in society, and data based innovation can generate business opportunities and ways to improve access to justice. Currently, clients ask lawyers for information and in many cases they get educated guesses on outcomes. These situations are high stakes for clients, and they need better data on probable outcomes (Walters 2018, 1–2). Even relatively small increases in the quality of information lawyers give clients lead to substantial improvements in the probable value that clients can antici- pate (Sutherland 2017). A longitudinal report published in 2019 found that the difference between the business statistics for successful and unsuccessful firms is very small, but the compounding effects of a few percentage points combine to flourishing or failing practices over time (Clio 2019). Improving data use to improve decision making can generate these changes.

There are important aspects of the legal industry that make data applications more complicated than they are in other disciplines. The law and legal organiza- tions have long histories — in many cases they outlive the jurisdictions that created them. For example, in Namibia there are acts that have origins in Dutch, English, South African, and Indigenous law, because the laws associated with different colonial and local governments were brought forward as time passed (Badeva- Bright 2021). On a smaller scale, many law firms continue in business over decades, and they need to make sure that the information they need from that whole period is available to them, from wills that were stored decades ago to the emails that may need to be included in e-discovery from last week.

Inclusion of that depth of history is imperative to handle the complexity of human communities and how they are governed. At the same time, law is ever changing, and any successful data driven system will have to accommodate these changes. The element of the passage of time in legal systems is imperative to understand, and it makes the analysis of legal data different from the analysis of scientific data. It would be as if scientific methodology required inclusion of a single body of data from past experiments going back centuries, but which is continually updated, for researchers to work in a contemporary lab.

Experts in law need to be involved in the development of projects from the beginning. It is common for software to be developed without the input of legal experts until the last stage when it is prohibitively expensive to make changes. In contrast, having legal input at the preliminary design stage makes integrating these considerations into systems comparatively cheap and easy (Walker 2019, 145).

1.3 Applications

There are so many possible ways for data to be used in legal scholarship and the legal industry that it is impossible to list them all here. The following sec- tions are intended to give an outline of some possibilities to help give context to coming the chapters.

Business improvement

One of the most relevant and easiest to implement ways to use legal data is through collecting and using data to improve business metrics within law firms, legal departments, and other legal businesses. This data can be collected and analyzed using well developed business techniques to develop performance in many ways. They can:

- Manage financial performance
- Increase productivity
- Improve client retention and acquisition
- Quantify the impacts of particular units or practice areas
- Measure the contributions of particular lawyers beyond billable hours

This can be as simple as being more careful about how website analytics are interpreted, but it can also become quite complex. Happily, practice management tools are starting to include better data recording and analysis functionality in their tools, so it is becoming easier to collect and use.

Legal research

Legal research has changed a great deal in the last thirty years as it has become digitized, and the majority of it is now done online. Part of the reason this took so long is that there was so much historical data that needed to be digitized in order to make the transition viable. This is still not complete, and anyone who is doing in depth historical legal research can expect to have to go to print volumes with some regularity, but for most questions online tools are sufficient now.

The big driver of methodological change until now has been search, with an ongoing shift from controlled vocabularies, taxonomies, and curated indices to more automated systems. Improved data techniques have certainly been instrumental in driving improvements in search and now machine learning is creating new generations of systems that integrate the data that years of use have generated.

Tools like machine learning are now taking this further. They are improving search by allowing for more flexible searches to be run from documents and longer texts rather than just from keywords. Search systems are getting better at delivering what researchers mean rather than just the results that follow from the direct terms entered. Now with systems like Google's search algorithm BERT, it is no longer necessary to include precise words that appear in results as it is efficient at searching for concepts regardless of vocabulary (Arredondo 2021).

Machine learning is also being used to automatically generate value added finding tools such as case summaries, classification, legal dictionaries, and annotated legislation. The ease of keyword searching has made these tools less popular with researchers in recent years, so it will be interesting to see how the social dynamics of adoption of these new tools changes as they become more cost effective, but they can be anticipated to be a focus of development in the foreseeable future.

The next segment of the legal research market that will likely develop and be widely adopted is writing assist software which will automatically generate document drafts based on inputs or do things like suggest the next clauses that can be included in contracts. These have existed for some time, but they will improve and become more accessible and cost effective.

Academic research

The possibilities for academic research driven by data analysis are substantial. There are many opportunities to explore techniques from other disciplines to understand the law and social aspects of legal systems. Researchers are particularly encouraged to increase their use of experimental methodologies such as randomized controlled testing to better quantify the impacts of different interventions (Lynch, Greiner, and Cohen 2020). Extensive research into free text analysis using case law and structural analysis of citation networks has also shown promising results. The adoption of these methodologies has been accelerating in recent years, but the limited availability of data and the issues with the data that is available has limited progress in many jurisdictions.

The levels of investment in making data available, privacy laws, and a lack of generally available datasets in countries like the United Kingdom, Canada, and Australia, contrasted with the relative ease of access to legal data in the United States and European Union, mean that there has been divergence in research activity. Data driven research in the United States and European Union is significantly further developed. This is to a large degree because the primary law datasets, such as case law, court dockets, and legislation, are more generally available. Over time, there will be room to move forward with increased research based on techniques drawn from many disciplines, such as law, computer science, information science, and criminology.

Court processes

Around the world there are already explorations into how to improve court processes to better serve communities. Court processes can be improved in many ways using technology applications:

- They can be designed to be more comprehensible to the parties who need justice.
- They can be designed to be more efficient, so that more matters can be processed in the same amount of time.

- They can be designed to be more fair, so people do not have different outcomes for inappropriate reasons like race, gender, or class.

And many other possibilities. Many court systems have had years of underinvestment in technology, and one hopes this will be an area of focus in the future. There is potential to make considerable improvements in how courts are run using methods like mapping processes from the perspective of people who have to navigate it and then simplifying them on the organizations' side so that they make sense to people (Salter 2021). Much of this work is not as data intensive as other uses for legal data but recording and using the data indicates what is needed.

Consumer focused applications

One of the most exciting opportunities in the coming years is the provision of data and programmatically driven applications that can be provided directly to consumers. There have been limits to the development and deployment of these applications because of different regulatory requirements around the world, data availability, and other constraints. However, there seems to be movement to relax some of these limitations. Legal regulators have started introducing initiatives like regulatory sandboxes, which allow for the relaxing of rules surrounding the development of legal businesses so that companies can experiment. These changes paired with technological improvements have the potential to provide services in many different practice areas, including:

- Wills and estates
- Family law
- Tax
- Dispute resolution

The benefit to the public from this shift is that many people who are poorly served by the current legal system will have the ability to get help. This is possible because many people's legal problems are simple from the perspective of someone who knows the law, but to them they are almost insurmountable.

The best way to use data in these applications is to create ways to scale processes to increase productivity. Routine matters can be dealt with easily and quickly with data driven services, and once the systems handle them well, it will be an incremental step to increase the complexity of the matters being handled. This is the most likely way that the existing legal industry will be disrupted, and the biggest barrier is the regulation of legal practice. It will be interesting to see how this proceeds in the coming years.

1.4 Sources

Different types of organizations have different contexts for the creation and use of data, as they all have different priorities and needs. Legal data can include many things, here are some examples that may be interesting to explore for data driven legal applications:

- Court judgements and dockets
- Legislation, including statutes, bills, codes, and regulations
- Documents generated by lawyers in their practices
- Academic research data
- Business data from legal technology companies and law firms

There are many more that may be possible sources. The important thing is to think critically about what the data is, how it is created, and what limitations it has before investing too heavily in developing systems to use it.

Courts and tribunals

Court and tribunal issued decisions have been some of the most commonly used sources of data for analysis. Whether this is because they are good sources of data for understanding issues or because they are generally publicly available and widely known is unclear. That said, they are an integral part of the law, and the processes leading up to and involved in litigation are extremely expensive and time consuming. If solutions could be found to help gain efficiency and help people understand the law and likely outcomes better, it would be a great help in this area.

Decisions

Court decisions are some of the most visible and widely accessed sources of data of the law. They are interesting because they are the result of the adjudication process with significant implications for the parties involved and society at large. They are in fact part of the law which has to be interpreted, though how much weight they have in future decision making varies depending on considerations like issuing body and jurisdiction. Extracting rules and precepts from case law is a challenge for human readers, and this has also proved to be difficult for computer systems. There is a clear use case for finding a better way to present the information they contain, though there are also legitimate concerns about what might be lost in that process.

Even where the data in case law is accessible, it is not possible to use it as a sole source of data to understand the process of litigation and dispute resolution in a jurisdiction. Court decisions are not representative of all the outcomes of matters that people and organizations experience. Instead they represent the outcomes of matters that went to trial and were sufficiently unusual for a judge to consider it necessary to issue a written opinion. Figure 1.1 shows the header of a court decision from the Supreme Court of Canada. It includes common formatting and content attributes, such as identifying parties' names, citation, and procedural information, and details about the subject matter.

[2009] 2 R.C.S.   R. c. GRANT   353

Donnohue Grant *Appellant*	**Donnohue Grant** *Appelant*
v.	*c.*
Her Majesty The Queen *Respondent*	**Sa Majesté la Reine** *Intimée*
and	et
Director of Public Prosecutions of Canada, Attorney General of British Columbia, Canadian Civil Liberties Association and Criminal Lawyers' Association (Ontario) *Interveners*	**Directeur des poursuites pénales du Canada, procureur général de la Colombie-Britannique, Association canadienne des libertés civiles et Criminal Lawyers' Association (Ontario)** *Intervenants*

INDEXED AS: R. v. GRANT

Neutral citation: 2009 SCC 32.

File No.: 31892.

2008: April 24; 2009: July 17.

Present: McLachlin C.J. and Binnie, LeBel, Deschamps, Fish, Abella and Charron JJ.

ON APPEAL FROM THE COURT OF APPEAL FOR ONTARIO

Constitutional law — Charter of Rights — Arbitrary detention — Right to counsel — Encounter between accused and police going from general neighbourhood policing to situation where police effectively took control over accused and attempted to elicit incriminating information — Whether police conduct would cause a reasonable person in accused's position to conclude that he or she was not free to go and had to comply with police demand — Whether accused arbitrarily detained — Meaning of "detention" in ss. 9 and 10 of Canadian Charter of Rights and Freedoms.

Constitutional law — Charter of Rights — Enforcement — Exclusion of evidence — Firearm discovered as result of accused's statements taken in breach of his right against arbitrary detention and right to counsel — Firearm admitted into evidence at trial and accused convicted of five firearms offences — Whether admission of firearm bringing administration of justice into

RÉPERTORIÉ : R. c. GRANT

Référence neutre : 2009 CSC 32.

Nᵒ du greffe : 31892.

2008 : 24 avril; 2009 : 17 juillet.

Présents : La juge en chef McLachlin et les juges Binnie, LeBel, Deschamps, Fish, Abella et Charron.

EN APPEL DE LA COUR D'APPEL DE L'ONTARIO

Droit constitutionnel — Charte des droits — Détention arbitraire — Droit à l'assistance d'un avocat — Contact entre l'accusé et les policiers relevant de services de police communautaire devenu un interrogatoire visant à obtenir des renseignements incriminants dans une situation où l'accusé était bel et bien contrôlé par les policiers — La conduite policière inciterait-elle une personne raisonnable placée dans la même situation que l'accusé à conclure qu'elle n'est pas libre de partir et qu'elle doit obtempérer à la sommation de la police? — L'accusé a-t-il été détenu arbitrairement? — A-t-il été porté atteinte au droit de l'accusé d'avoir recours à l'assistance d'un avocat? — Sens du mot « détention » pour l'application des art. 9 et 10 de la Charte canadienne des droits et libertés.

Droit constitutionnel — Charte des droits — Réparation — Exclusion d'éléments de preuve — Arme à feu découverte par suite de déclarations de l'accusé obtenues en violation de ses droits de ne pas être détenu arbitrairement et d'avoir recours à l'assistance d'un avocat — Arme à feu utilisée en preuve au procès et accusé déclaré coupable de cinq infractions relatives

2009 SCC 32 (CanLII)

Figure 1.1 The header of a court decision from the Supreme Court of Canada. Reproduced under Reproduction of Federal Law Order (SI/97–5)

DOCKETS

Docket filings are the documents that are filed with the court in the process of litigation. They often have more detailed information about facts and process than judges' written decisions, and there are significantly more of them than there are written decisions. This makes them an attractive target for machine learning and court outcome prediction, especially when they are paired with the decisions. However, dockets are not available from all courts and tribunals in a readily accessible format, because of issues like lack of investment in court computing infrastructure and privacy concerns. Privacy is particularly important with docket information, because of the detailed information about individuals and events they contain. If these issues can be overcome and academic and industry researchers can get access to docket filings to use in their work, it has the potential to generate a great deal of insight into the justice system and how it can be improved.

COURT BUSINESS DATA

Like other organizations that deal with large numbers of documents, staff, and external stakeholders, courts and tribunals generate a large amount of data in their business processes which can be integrated into analyses and applications. This could be used to identify areas for possible efficiencies, identify issues, and otherwise improve court processes.

Legislative bodies

Legislative or parliamentary bodies, such as Congress in the United States or the Houses of Parliament in the United Kingdom, are the other major component of law making. Legislative bodies have prescribed processes for passing laws, which involve requirements for things like reading bills or proposed laws before the members in the house a certain number of times, and debates or other exploration of their potential impacts, before they are approved through a vote by elected representatives to become legislation. These processes creates significant bodies of documents at each stage, which have the potential to be used as data sources. In addition to the documents themselves, it is common for statistical data about the process and voting histories to be used as a significant source of data to understand the process and politicians' behavior better.

In common law jurisdictions it is common for there to be more focus on case law as a target for data analysis than legislation, but legislation is a significant potential data source in its own right. There is variation in how legislation fits into the system: legislation, in civil law jurisdictions in the form of civil codes, is more central to the law than it is in common law jurisdictions in civil law jurisdictions. There are positives and negatives to using legislation for analysis:

- It may be easier to access legislative data than case law as it generally has no personally identifiable information, which can raise concerns about wider distribution of datasets.
- Legislation is often available in more standardized formats and in smaller numbers of documents, which makes it easier to prepare for use.
- Legislation is regularly amended, and these changes can be significant — in fact whole documents can be repealed or added from one day to the next. Whereas generally case law is added to but once it is issued individual documents are more consistent over time.

Legislation typically includes statutes or chapters, codes, and regulations. Statutes or chapters are the ongoing laws that govern particular topics. They may be introduced and passed as complete documents, or particular sections may be amended by other statutes. Some statutes are entirely made up of amendments to other statutes. This complexity means that generally they are published as consolidations, which give the text of statutes as they are at any particular time. Civil codes are a different format of legislation which include compiled accounts of the law. They are updated as the law changes. There are many civil codes used around the world, notable examples include the *United States Code* and the French *Code Civil*. Figure 1.2 shows an example of a statute as published by the Scottish Parliament. It includes common formatting attributes for statutes, though details vary by jurisdiction.

Criminal Justice (Scotland) Act 2016 (asp 1)

Criminal Justice (Scotland) Act 2016
2016 asp 1

CONTENTS

Figure 1.2 The title page of a statute from Scottish Parliament. Contains public sector information licensed under the Open Government Licence v3.0

Regulations are the detailed documents which give precise instructions on how statutes or codes should be applied, and they can be described as secondary legislation. The authority to issue regulations is typically specified in statutes or codes and government bodies such as government departments issue them based on that delegated authority. Generally, details of how the laws will be interpreted and enforced like numbers, particular places, and organizations appear only in regulations.

Government departments

Many governments have started publishing their data in ways that make it freely available for analysis, referred to as open data. Much of this data has nothing to do with the law, but some justice related information is often included, and what is there can be integrated with other data sources to create valuable insights. Frequently this data is published in online open data portals in various formats. The most common open data that may be of interest in law is statistical information about the justice system. In addition to open data, governments also publish many documents. These may include substantial data driven analysis, but whether the supporting data is also available varies by government and topic. Newer content is more likely to have the data available.

Law firms and lawyers

Lawyers and other law firm staff generate substantial amounts of data in the course of their work. This includes things like:

- Legal research and analysis
- Interpretations of and opinions on the law
- Other documents
- Data about business processes

This data has the potential to be source of substantial competitive advantage if it is collected and interpreted well. One of the potential advantages of being in a large firm is the way people can learn from each other and raise the level of all their performances through shared knowledge that can be generated by having many people together. However, if there are not those economies of learning, then there may not be as much justification to pay the higher fees that large firms charge.

Going forward, there will be software applications that allow law firms' data to be collected and used in more dynamic ways. This will make it significantly easier to assess aspects of lawyers' work and businesses. The documents lawyers generate in their work are another significant source of data that can be used to understand processes better and to develop systems to assist in document creation in the future.

Academic research

Academic research in law and other disciplines such as criminology and computer science has been an important driver in the development of the understanding of legal data. This research tends not to be on the leading edge of what the technologies can do, but there has been a lot of work that has used techniques developed in other fields and then used on legal data. The technological developments that tend to be most important for analyses of law have to do with the size and complexity of the documents involved, as legal documents have substantial size and complexity. This is valuable because it provides new insights into the law and legal processes.

Some examples of applications that have emerged from academic research in this field include applications that use law as code and law as data. Law as code applications include tax software and applications in family law. Law as data applications include e-discovery, case outcome prediction, and search (Frankenreiter and Livermore 2019, 23).

Legal technology companies

There has been a great deal of activity in the legal technology space in the last decade. The legal industry represents an enormous market that many believe could be served better or disrupted, and startups and investors want to move into the space. Many of these companies use data in various ways to drive their systems. The availability of data to drive startups' applications has been an issue in some jurisdictions, depending on what kinds of data they want to use.

1.5 Global context

Around the world there is variation in what data is available, how it can be used, and how much work has already been done in the area of legal data development and analysis. These differences are based on many things, including privacy laws, legacy investment in systems, legal publishing norms, legal regulation, and culture. The following national and regional summaries are intended to give context for some of the discussions in subsequent chapters and give some additional information about how legal data is approached in their parts of the world and how it compares with others. It is not possible to be exhaustive in a book of this size, and examples from other countries may be mentioned in other chapters as they are relevant.

United States

The United States is one of the major centers of innovation in legal data analysis research and commercialization in the world. In particular, it has a longer tradition of quantitative analysis of case law than other countries. There are several areas of law that have standardized datasets available for research, such as sentencing, and there are ongoing commitments to record statistical information (Frug 2021). Partly this is because it is a center of development for the commercialization of new technology generally, and the critical mass of innovation in research and start up hubs like Silicon Valley means that there is energy for development of possibilities.

There are less stringent privacy restrictions for access to and publication of case law in the United States than there are in many other countries, so it is possible to do things with it that may be restricted or forbidden in other jurisdictions. Compared to other common law countries there has been better availability of case law for analysis, and it is a large country with a large collection of law for use in machine learning, which has made more development possible.

Historical and cultural attitudes around the publication of law are important factors in the availability of primary law for analysis, and the United States have a stronger tradition of commercial access to law than many other countries do. There is a common acceptance that the law is something that it is acceptable to commercialize, which affects how the law can be accessed. In fact there are many states that do not provide full free access to their laws online (Glassmeyer 2014). That said, there are also many non-profit providers of legal information which are working to improve access and legal challenges have been made where certain activities are prohibited. Like in other countries, the different formats and standards that each court uses in preparing their documents means that creating a single document database is a significant undertaking.

Canada

In Canada there is limited access to primary law for data analysis. Some provincial and Federal legislation is available as open data in Canada, but generally courts and governments have not chosen to make case law widely available for analysis. Canadian government publications are protected by Crown Copyright, where the government holds copyright for that content, how this affects primary law is under debate. There have been cases brought before Canadian privacy commissioners and the Federal Court of Canada regarding the republication of case law and the privacy interests individuals have in these public documents that nevertheless have significant personal information in them (Complaints against Globe24h.com 2015, A.T. v. Globe24h.com 2017). Law firms and academic researchers are developing expertise and systems to better use data, and it can be anticipated that this will be an area of growth in coming years.

United Kingdom

The United Kingdom has seen less activity in legal data from academic researchers than the United States, though this is starting to change. Partly this is because the primary law has been less generally available for analysis. It is still unclear where intellectual property rights in case law reside (Winterton 2021). Though data protection laws in the United Kingdom are required to comply with European Union legislation, particularly the *General Data Protection Regulation (GDPR)*, the *Data Protection Act 2018* includes an exemption for information associated with legal proceedings. Coverage of case law has been an ongoing issue as the feeds that publishers get is truncated based on what judges decide is important enough to send for publication (Winterton 2021). Significant portions of court processes are still paper based, and this limits the ability to develop data based understanding of decision making in both criminal and civil matters (Hoadley 2021).

There are now several projects being carried out by academic researchers looking to apply artificial intelligence to law. Researchers exploring artificial intelligence applications in United Kingdom law explicitly take into account the idea that it is designed to be competitive internationally, and that it draws business and opportunities from abroad (University of Oxford Faculty of Law 2018). Law firms in the United Kingdom are regarded as being particularly sophisticated in their use of data in their practices.

European Union

The European Union is an interesting region for the purposes of legal data because many countries there have some of the most extensive access to primary law from government sources of anywhere in the world. This is paired with some of the world's strictest privacy and data protection laws. This is achieved by anonymizing all case law before publication, so it can be made easily available to researchers and companies. Governments in the European Union have also invested heavily in exploring innovative ways to publish the laws electronically and have made extensive investment in technology platforms. They are global leaders in this area.

Though there are many similarities across the European Union, there is still significant variation within it, with France in particular taking a different direction than other countries. In 2019, France passed a law forbidding the publication of statistical analysis of judicial activities (Légifrance 2019). The motivations for this law are not clear, but there is some speculation that it includes issues of privacy for the judges and potential visibility of deviation from norms (Artificial Lawyer 2019).

Africa

It is difficult to discuss a continent as large and diverse as Africa together, but in Africa there are shared actors and issues in the fields associated with legal data that make this more sensical than it might seem. For simplicity, this summary is focused on the countries in Africa with common law traditions. There are several organizations providing access to African law headquartered in South Africa.

As is the case elsewhere, legal systems reflect African history, which means that knowledge of that history continues to be necessary to understand the current environment and legal structures. For example, there are important regional aspects of how the laws have been passed and administered; until the 1980s there was an East African Court of Appeal that served Kenya, Uganda and Tanzania, and that was one dataset, and in Lesotho, 19th century English laws are still part of the statute book, because they were never converted into Lesotho laws in the same way they were in many other countries with colonial histories (Badeva-Bright 2021). Ongoing access to primary law generally continues to be an issue with technological limitations, such as interrupted email service, frequently interfering with to ability of courts to send decisions for publication (Pillay 2021).

It can be hoped that moving from primarily print to primarily online publication of laws after standards have already been developed elsewhere will allow the legal data landscape in Africa to develop quickly as investments are made. Significant work is being done to develop data based applications and initiatives that will allow for better access to legal documents.

India

The availability of Indian primary law has increased greatly in recent years, and at the time of writing several new start-ups have emerged in the space in the last four to five years. The law is available on publicly accessible sites, but not to the degree that might be expected based on India's size — current government policy has emphasized business interests over public access, which has limited development in this space (Vivekanandan 2021). There has been a push to increase the use of data driven applications to increase efficiency. It was reported in 2019 that only 4% of Indian lawyers were using artificial intelligence applications, which was significantly less than in other countries. According to the chief justice, Indian courts have been working with artificial intelligence to support case and data management (Hebbar 2019). Partly the speed adoption has been limited by the lack of data to build applications (Yolmo 2019).

Singapore

Singapore is an interesting example of what can happen if a government is willing to invest heavily in developing capacity in legal computing and data use and has sufficient existing infrastructure to make it happen. The main source for Singaporean primary law is LawNet, a paid service run by the Singapore Academy of Law, and because they own the data, they have the ability to allow research and other uses. Singaporean law is a relatively small dataset with approximately 10,000 decisions being issued by the courts since independence in 1965, and approximately 2,000 more if decisions related to Singaporean matters from the Privy Council and other sources are included. These conditions combine to mean that generally Singaporean primary law is quite accessible for use (Soh 2021). The Singaporean government is putting resources into encouraging technology adoption in the legal sector (Artificial Lawyer 2019). Singapore has different issues for data analysis than other countries due to its small size (Soh, Lim, and Chai 2019). The research being done there to address this in Singapore may have important implications for other countries with smaller datasets.

Australia

Australia has many similar issues to other countries discussed here. Australian law is covered by crown copyright which can limit access for reuse of data, though some jurisdictions are open to the idea of using open licenses such as those provided by Creative Commons for legislation. Australian governments and courts are still developing ways of navigating how to decide when to make primary law available for reuse as data. As in other countries, there are ongoing issues with private information being included in court documents, which limit their reuse in data applications (Mobray and Chung 2021).

1.6 Conclusion

Understanding data will allow better understanding of what kind of data can be found, created, or captured, and when it is appropriate or inappropriate to use it. Not every situation lends itself to automated data analysis: it is frequently more efficient to have a person review case law manually than set up a machine learning instance. But other applications like e-discovery generally have sufficient scale that they reward these techniques. Many people have described data as the "new oil" (Frey 2019, 304). This analogy has limits, but there are substantial opportunities to improve understanding. The coming chapters will explain the issues and opportunities associated with legal data and give a starting off point for future exploration.

Works cited

Arredondo, Pablo. 2021. (Co-Founder and Chief Product Officer at Casetext), in conversation with the author.

Artificial Lawyer. 2019. "Singapore Gov Subsidises Costs of Law Firm Tech Adoption." *Artificial Lawyer* (blog). May 9, 2019. https://www.artificiallawyer.com/2019/05/09/singapore-gov-subsidises-costs-of-law-firm-tech-adoption/.

A.T. v. Globe24h.com. 2017 2017 FC 114 (CanLII), [2017] 4 FCR 310. Federal Court.

Badeva-Bright, Mariya. 2021. (Co-founder Laws.Africa and Project Director AfricanLII, University of Cape Town), in discussion with the author.

Clio. 2019. "2019 Legal Trends Report." Burnaby, Canada: Clio. https://www.clio.com/resources/legal-trends/2019-report/read-online/.

Complaints against Globe24h.com. 2015 2015 CanLII 33260 (PCC). Privacy Commissioner of Canada.

Frankenreiter, Jens, and Michael A. Livermore. 2019. "Computational Methods in Legal Analysis." SSRN Scholarly Paper ID 3568558. Rochester, NY: Social Science Research Network. https://papers.ssrn.com/abstract=3568558.

Frey, Carl Benedikt. 2019. *The Technology Trap: Capital, Labor, and Power in the Age of Automation.* Princeton, NJ: Princeton University Press.

Frug, Sara. 2021. (Co-Director at Legal Information Institute), in conversation with the author.

Glassmeyer, Sarah. 2014. "State Legal Information Census: An Analysis of Primary State Legal Information." http://www.sarahglassmeyer.com/StateLegalInformation/wp-con tent/uploads/2014/04/GlassmeyerStateLegalInformationCensusReport.pdf.

Hebbar, Prajakta. 2019. "CJI Bobde Says AI Won't Be Used for Decision-Making in Supreme Court." *Analytics India Magazine* (blog). December 16, 2019. https://ana lyticsindiamag.com/cji-bobde-says-ai-will-not-be-used-for-decision-making-in-supreme-court-but-for-case-management/.

Hoadley, Daniel. 2021. (Head of Litigation Data at Mishcon de Reya LLP), in discussion with the author.

Légifrance. "Article 33 - LOI N° 2019-222 Du 23 Mars 2019 de Programmation 2018-2022 et de Réforme Pour La Justice (1)." Légifrance, March 24, 2019. https://www.legifrance.gouv.fr/eli/loi/2019/3/23/JUST1806695L/jo/article_33.

Lynch, H. Fernandez, D. J. Greiner, and I. G. Cohen. 2020. "Overcoming Obstacles to Experiments in Legal Practice." *Science* 367 (6482): 1078–1080. https://doi.org/10.1126/science.aay3005.

Mobray, Andrew, and Philip Chung. 2021. (Co-Director and Executive Director AustLII [Australasian Legal Information Institute]), in discussion with the author.

Pillay, Carina. 2021. (Project Director SAFLII [Southern African Legal Information Institute]), in discussion with the author.

Salter, Shannon. 2021. (Chair at Civil Resolution Tribunal of British Columbia, and adjunct professor at the UBC Allard School of Law), in discussion with the author.

Soh, Jerrold. 2021. (Assistant Professor of Law and Deputy Director, Centre for Computational Law at the Singapore Management University), in discussion with the author.

Soh, Jerrold, How Khang Lim, and Ian Ernst Chai. 2019. "Legal Area Classification: A Comparative Study of Text Classifiers on Singapore Supreme Court Judgments." In *Proceedings of the Natural Legal Language Processing Workshop 2019*, 67–77. Minneapolis, Minnesota: Association for Computational Linguistics. https://doi.org/10.18653/v1/W19-2208.

Sutherland, Sarah. 2017. "Quantifying the Value of Legal Information." *Slaw* (blog). June 1, 2017. http://www.slaw.ca/2017/06/01/quantifying-the-value-of-legal-information/.

University of Oxford Faculty of Law. 2018. "Unlocking the Potential of Artificial Intelligence for English Law." December 20, 2018. https://www.law.ox.ac.uk/unlocking-p otential-artificial-intelligence-english-law.

Vivekanandan, V. C. 2021. (Vice Chancellor at Hidayatullah National Law University), in discussion with the author.

Walker, Joshua. 2019. *On Legal AI.* Washington, DC: Full Court Press.

Walters, Edward. 2018. "Introduction: Data Analytics for Law Firms: Using Data for Smarter Legal Services." In *Data-Driven Law: Data Analytics and the New Legal Services*, edited by Edward Walters, 1–10. Boca Raton, FL: Auerbach Publications.

Winterton, Jules. 2021. (Chief Executive Officer, British and Irish Legal Information Institute (BAILII)), in discussion with the author.

Yolmo, Yeshey Rabzyor. 2019. "Why Do Only 4% of Indian Lawyers Use AI, Even Though 95% of the Courts Are Digitised?" *Analytics India Magazine*. December 27, 2019. https://analyticsindiamag.com/legal-tech/.

Chapter 2

Sources of data

2.1 Introduction

There are many types of data that can be used to illustrate the law, legal system, and how people interact with it, and there are just as many sources for it. Primary law collections, such as court cases and legislation, are some of the most obvious datasets to be used as legal data, and potential sources for them include courts, legislative bodies, government printers, and publishers depending on the jurisdiction. It can also include the data generated in the operations of legal organizations and businesses, such as law firms, ministries of justice, and courts. Legal data frequently overlaps with the data used in related disciplines like criminology, social work, and other social sciences. Suitable sources for this kind of data may be available from government agencies or other sources such as university researchers.

That said, this data may not be easy to access. Sourcing it is one of the most complicated elements of integrating data driven insights into legal scholarship and practice. In fact, there are significant limits to accessing both private and public documents for use as data in many countries, particularly primary law. These limits may be frustrating to those who want to work in this space, but the issues associated with access, notably technical limitations, privacy concerns, and sometimes intellectual property considerations, can be substantial. Intellectual property rights in primary law for example is highly jurisdiction specific, and even where intellectual property law allows for the use of the data, it still may still not be available. Many governments and courts have not invested in developing systems that support this type of use.

Beyond the technical and legal limits, in many cases there are in fact still substantial gaps in what content is available in electronic formats at all. Though it might seem that courts and governments would make their documents and other data available for analysis, in many jurisdictions this is simply not the case.

Case law and other documents associated with adjudication in particular can be sensitive, and fixes that may seem simple, like anonymization of parties' names, are not always practicable or sufficient. Many courts lack sufficient resources to

DOI: 10.4324/9781003127307-2

anonymize judgements before they are sent to publishers, and anonymization has limits, especially since re-identification research shows that it is often possible to link people's identities with the data about them without much difficulty. Even simple reading of a decision may be enough for someone familiar with the facts to identify individuals: in small communities in particular it is difficult to ensure that it is not possible to identify parties to litigation (Mobray and Chung 2021). While primary law is usually available for use in legal research, re-publishers of the law in particular are often conservative about providing it in bulk to third parties for different uses than those for which it was originally supplied (Winterton 2021).

Some sources of data are openly available, while others are available by subscription, and some are internal to organizations. Each of these can tell researchers different things, and sometimes they can be combined to give more specific insights. However, there are significant holes in what legal data is available, and it may be necessary to find ways to collect the data to fill a need rather than access an existing dataset.

Even where data is accessible, most legal data is generated for a particular purpose, which may be adjudication, communicating the law, or as the result of activities like business processes or web traffic. These datasets may not be the best data for driving applications and analyses. This means that large organizations like governments, big commercial publishers, and large law firms, have significant advantages, because they can create their own data systems and can design how it will be collected and administered. Many start up companies looking to operate in the legal technology space focus on developing their algorithms as the priority for how to move forward and pay significantly less attention to the data they use to populate it, which can severely limit the quality of their offerings (Winterton 2021).

Part of the problem is that frequently existing data is incomplete: "In many legal contexts an outcome variable like reoffending is not available: there often is no better indicator for the right decision than the one that was made" (Copus, Hübert, and Laqueur 2019, 48). This means that there is no data available that can be used to train applications like machine learning systems to give socially optimal outcomes. Existing biases and injustices are carried forward to these new systems, and if this problem is not solved, these issues will get worse as tools like decision recommenders become more widespread.

To improve this situation, it seems inevitable that going forward data analysis and creation will become more intimately integrated into the processes of law and governance. It will be interesting to see how this is done, and how much the needs of data based applications will drive the design of legal processes, and how much this could impinge on other values that could dictate how they are designed instead.

2.2 Sources

There are many sources of data on legal systems and outcomes. These can be relatively straightforward, such as regulations as a source for understanding governance of industry or statistical information about court processes. However, even where data is clearly related to a particular topic, it may be difficult to parse and analyze. Other sources of data are less straightforward, and it can be very difficult to know how to find data that will illuminate quantitative questions that seem like they should have answers:

> measuring whether a crime has occurred is not a straight forward matter. It requires relying on officially recorded criminal justice events, such as a crime report, an arrest, a conviction, or a return to prison, none of which may be consistent proxies for criminal behavior.
> (Copus, Hübert, and Laqueur 2019, 50)

These questions and others may not have quantitative answers available, and qualitative answers from participants in the justice system often contain bias (Salter 2021).

Sourcing data to find answers to questions can be as much a matter of creativity and insight as it is a matter of logic and accuracy, but there are usually some sources of data available. What follows is an overview of many of the kinds of data sources that may be accessible, with some description of how these processes work. Please keep in mind that it will be necessary to check how things are handled locally before committing resources to a project.

Governments

Governments around the world have been making more data available in recent years, especially statistical data. Some of this is open data, which researchers can access and use with limited restrictions. While some has more restrictions and may require agreements with government agencies, or it may not be available for researchers to use at all.

Open datasets

Many governments make data available with open licenses and in formats that are conducive for analysis and development. Though they may not be as open with regard to either license or format as potential users may wish, these datasets represent an important move toward openness and a meaningful improvement in accessibility of data about the workings of government and society. For example, the Government of Canada has had an open by default policy since 2016 (Treasury Board of Canada Secretariat 2019), and many other governments have similar policies. The most commonly discussed open datasets about ten years ago were things like municipal garbage pick-up schedules, but the complexity of the available data has increased in recent years and may include data about the legal system and even electronic copies of laws. Typically, any data that includes information with privacy, national security, or solicitor-client privilege implications is removed before publication. Case law is typically not made available in this way.

Parliamentary bodies

Typically, parliamentary bodies pass laws, which have names like statutes, acts, or chapters. These are classified as primary legislation. In some justice systems, these documents are then brought together in codes, which give a consolidated version of all the primary legislation in that category, such as the *United States Code* or the *French Civil Code*. This primary legislation gives high level direction for governance.

The process of publishing the laws may be considerably more complicated in some jurisdictions than others. In the United States, there is a mix of positive laws, which are statutes that have been passed by legislative bodies directly, and non-positive laws, which are codified compilations of positive laws, but which did not go through the legislative process in that form. This makes it more complicated to know where to find the law than it may be in other jurisdictions as it is not consistent, and many people needing regular access to statutes maintain them manually as they are updated (Frug 2021). These kinds of jurisdiction specific irregularities are important considerations when accessing legislation and should be investigated locally to ensure that correct assumptions are being made about the structure of the documents.

Individual acts or chapters may also include text delegating the power to develop regulations to other organizations like government agencies, which contain detailed guidance on how the law will be implemented. This is referred to as secondary legislation. Both primary and secondary legislation are updated regularly.

In addition to these final documents, there are also many documents that are created in the process of developing and passing legislation:

- Proposed legislation as it is read in the house, typically these documents will be in three versions, with the last version being the one that is voted on and which becomes law if it passes
- Transcripts of the debates in the house when legislation is being proposed
- Documents prepared by or for committees formed to make recommendations to the government
- Other documents such as informational sheets prepared for legislators

Depending on what researchers want to know, these other datasets may be better sources of information than the legislation itself. Unstructured text such as debates and committee transcripts are a richer record of the process of making law than structured text is (Eidelman, Kornilova, and Argyle 2019).

Many jurisdictions are exploring ways to make legislation available to support analysis and the development of better understanding and access. This can include many things, such as improving the data standards for how the data is published and making it available as downloadable files with fewer restrictions on use. In the long run legislation may be redesigned to be more machine readable.

Courts

Courts are a separate branch of government from parliamentary bodies. Simplistically, they interpret and apply the law, including both legislation and court and tribunal decisions, and decide how it will be applied in particular instances. Their interpretation is then usually published in the form of written documents, which may be called judgments, cases, or decisions. These then become part of the law and can feed into other court cases and, less frequently, initiate legislative changes. As this happens, the law grows and evolves as the process proceeds over time.

Court data can include the documents written and submitted by litigating parties. These are commonly referred to as pleadings, dockets, or court filings. It can also include business data about the courts' operations such as qualitative and quantitative data about court processes and the experiences of participants.

The availability of court data is affected by the local laws, organizational will, and technical capacity in each jurisdiction. Many researchers see case law and pleadings as a ready source of documents that can be accessed and used for data analytics, but for many reasons they can be one of the more problematic data sources to access. See Table 2.1 for some examples of qualitative and quantitative data that can be used to understand court processes.

Case law

Case law is the actual written documents released by courts which communicate their decisions. Collections of case law may be more or less complete

Table 2.1 Qualitative and quantitative data that can be collected about adjudicative processes

Examples of qualitative data:	• Data about participant satisfaction • Passive feedback • Rating buttons • Text boxes where people can ask for help • Information collected by front line staff
Examples of quantitative data:	• The number of cases • Stages where people drop off • How much processes cost • Participant satisfaction rates (Salter 2021)

depending on many issues which are mainly driven by decisions made within the courts. Judges have a great deal of discretion in how they write and issue their decisions, and this variability means that they can be quite difficult to manage in systematic ways. There have been calls for court decisions to be more structured in order to better support automation, but this approach has not been widely adopted.

Case law is one of the most common and most contentious data sources. It is comprised of public documents, but they may contain extensive information about the parties involved. This limits publication of court decisions as datasets for reuse in many places. In some countries, such as Austria, personal information is removed from court judgements before publication. In others it is not, which has given rise to debate about how litigants' and witnesses' personal information can be protected in an environment where court documents are generally available online (Bailey and Burkell 2017).

Many researchers look to case law for information about how disputes are handled or what happens to people in particular situations, but there are issues with using it to understand community dynamics. Most people in these situations do not go to court, and many of those who do settle their disputes before a judge issues a decision. Typically, cases settle based on attributes that are not random: the most simple, uncontentious, and routine matters are more likely to settle. This means there are significant issues with data distribution and sampling that need to be addressed before case law can be used extensively in developing solutions that try to give insights into these processes.

Case law is indicative of how judges decide in the subset of issues that appear before them, and which are sufficiently complicated or contentious that the litigants do not settle before a judgment is issued. Even among decisions that do get decided by a judge, there may still not be written decisions available: many decisions are only released orally, especially in routine issues, which means that the judge will say the decision aloud in court. These are frequently kept as audio recordings and only transcribed if someone is willing to pay for a private transcription, and often these recordings are not readily available to the public. This means that sourcing court decisions as data requires some sophistication regarding what is being requested.

There have also been significant changes over time to the ways court decisions are decided and published. When case law started being published online it was often delivered by the courts to publishers on floppy disks (Mobray and Chung 2021). This technological and process legacy cannot be ignored, as the history of how datasets were compiled affects the analyses that can be done with them.

In the last twenty years, there has been a reduction in the proportion of law that is public, because the number of disputes settled out of court has been increasing since the end of the 20th century. The high costs of litigation mean that parties more frequently resolve disputes using mechanisms like arbitration instead of litigation, which makes the result a private agreement, and the details of these settlements are generally not made public. This privatization means that it is difficult for anyone to access data about disputes' outcomes except for the parties involved (Grady 2018, 20–21).

There are different conditions in each jurisdiction that require some research to understand, but here are examples of some more detail for two places. Daniel Hoadley discussed the dynamics of this in the United Kingdom in 2018, finding that open access to case law is limited by the structure of the system for commercial contracts for the production of written transcripts. Many judgments, even important ones from superior courts, are only issued orally, and they are only available from commercial publishers that pay to have access to the transcripts (Hoadley 2018). In the United States, the existing datasets available for appellate decisions tend to only include written decisions, and even where they do include oral decisions they under represent particular types of matters like immigration appeals. Including oral decisions in a dataset adds significant complexity to the data acquisition process (Carlson, Livermore, and Rockmore 2020, 225), but it may be necessary to get good results.

Dockets

Dockets or court pleadings are the documents that are presented to the court as part of the litigation process. They are available for a wider selection of cases than judgements are because almost everything that has any litigation associated with it will have something filed with the courts, but for many reasons most of these matters will not end up having a written decision associated with them. There are many reasons why matters may be represented in court dockets but not judgments:

- The parties may have reached a private agreement
- The case could have been dismissed
- One of the parties could have missed a limitation deadline

Moreover, it is not always possible to know the outcomes associated with the dockets: if a case is settled between the parties or is simply dropped, there may be no detailed indication of the outcome in the court records.

Dockets represent a more detail rich data source for analysis than case law, but as datasets they still have significant technical limitations in addition to the process limitations discussed above. In many jurisdictions they may not be available electronically. In which case, though they are generally officially public, the fact that it is not possible to access them without physically going to a courthouse and requesting access to a paper file is a significant impediment to their use. Even where they are available electronically, it is common for them to only be available as scanned PDFs. This makes them almost as inaccessible as paper files for the purposes of analysis.

Business processes

Business processes in organizations like law firms, government agencies, and non-profits, are some of the most valuable sources of data in any organization, but in many cases there has not been good technical infrastructure that would allow this data to be extracted and analyzed. In recent years, new legal practice management software is being developed and adopted, which makes using this data much easier. Other legal organizations like ministries of justice are also improving their access to their own data and moving toward it can anticipate that many will have more data driven approaches to decision making.

As these systems become more widely available and integrated into operations, this will be a substantial new source of value generation for legal organizations, as it will allow them to better understand their operations and make evidence based decisions. This is important because understanding the organization itself and how it operates can be one of the biggest blind spots for any organization. The primary generators of value in these organization are not technological systems but people's efforts and insights. Understanding those people and the value they generate individually and in groups is an important element of data driven management.

Law firms and legal departments are sitting on piles of business and client data. However, it is generally unstructured, spread over multiple places, and often people do not know where it is. That said once firms realize how much data there is and how valuable it can be, it seems inevitable that they will start using it to validate business decisions. One example of a big source of valuable data that is unique to a particular firm is the data associated with settlements and deals that are never made public. Court judgements are generally fairly well structured and people are used to using them, but internal data can be a real competitive advantage because it is not publicly available (Hodgins 2021).

There are many potential ways data can be used to develop value for organizations, for example, a law firm could look at internal expertise by taking all the contracts from securities filings prepared by firms' members and assess people's actual skills based on what they have done and its quality (Jayasuriya 2018, 195). For a smaller firm, it may make more sense to do something like this manually as a big data process may not be efficient for a smaller dataset, but the technique matters less than looking for ways to validate or invalidate assumptions. The important thing is to consider what makes sense in a particular organization.

It is vital to make a plan for how data will be managed. In a law firm this should include planning to collect and use data to understand the following:

- Client inputs
- Nonclient inputs
- Public inputs
- Created data

- Public outputs
- Nonclient outputs
- Client outputs (Grady 2018, 24)

The increase in publicly available data combined with improved access to business data made available through improved software and good data creation practices means that even small organizations and solo practitioners can develop sophisticated data tools if that is something they want to invest in building (Grady 2018, 24).

Billing

One of the most common discussions in how law firms do business has been in the area of billing. The use of hourly billing creates disincentives to develop efficient ways of working, and many clients want better information about how much a matter is going to cost when a lawyer is hired. In many cases, lawyers have been hesitant to give firm quotes because they see too much variability in how much time handling individual matters takes. Better data collection and analysis allows for improved certainty on how to answer these questions confidently.

To get the data needed in an ongoing and dynamic way requires the following:

- A method of collection such as a suitable software system
- A plan for what data is required to understand what management wants to know
- A strategy for how to train firm members on how to record the data appropriately

It would also be possible to collate this data manually for a small firm, but this is labor intensive and the results would likely not be updated as regularly as in an automated process.

Collecting this data is labor intensive, so having a plan to assess how to use it and how to communicate its importance before the investment is made into collecting it is essential. Keep in mind that billing data is collected already as part of firms' regular business processes, so the behavior required should not be as different for firm members as it might be for people working in different industries who might have to start recording time. This means the incremental investment required to start collecting data strategically is less for law firms than it would be for many other kinds of businesses, so the balance of benefits to costs is greater.

This data can help a law firm answer questions beyond thinking in terms of how to bill clients more efficiently. It can help answer questions like what areas of practice are most profitable, who is writing off the most time, and what kinds of clients and practice areas are most likely to have higher long term value.

Web logs

One of the most common sources of data organizations have access to is web logs. Most organizations have websites, and they are frequently one of those organizations' most important marketing tools. This means that regardless of the organization, it is likely possible to improve outcomes based on website performance.

The use of website statistics should go beyond simple metrics like the number of visits to the site, as these primarily serve the purpose of providing an easily comparable number that people understand. They are often called vanity metrics. Instead, strategize as to what organizations want to achieve and how the site is used as a cue to what can be improved. Here are some examples of ways to target goals that could be improved by changes to an organizations' website:

- Track the percent of visitors to the site who navigate to the contact us page as a way to gauge how likely they are to want to pursue a working relationship
- Track the number of people going to the contact page compared to how many calls and emails come in to understand how potential clients want to communicate
- Track the behavior of visitors from different IP ranges associated with particular groups, such as exploring how visitors from law schools interact with the website to better understand topics like hiring dynamics
- Look at the organizations representing the top visitors to your website to look for potential clients or collaborators

Web logs are some of the easiest data sources to get started with because almost every organization has them. Beginning a data program using data that already exists is easier and gives the potential for early wins that can help an organization decide if more data analytics would be useful and if anyone internally has, or is interested in developing, the expertise to make a program like this work.

Legal publishers and data providers

Legal publishers have been slow to provide access to data as part of their product offerings, but this is changing. Published data may be sufficient to provide what is needed for a project itself, but it can also supplement business process and government data to allow for more complex analyses. Publishers may be more open to providing access to data to academic researchers than others, but they have overall been resistant to providing access to their full collections for analysis.

Publishers have been major innovators in the field of bringing data driven applications into the legal sector by integrating them into their products. Some of these, such as artificial intelligence driven brief generators, are overtly driven by data based tools. Others are less obviously data driven, such as when publishers integrate data based methodologies into their internal work processes to replace the work of human editors. Machine learning even makes it possible for publishers to capture users' behavior to contribute to their sites' functionality: each time a search is run and a particular result clicked on it could be used to improve the search results and responsiveness of the site (Nayyer 2021).

Many publishers also provide tools like data analytics platforms, which allow researchers to integrate insights from data analysis into their decision making, especially in the litigation process. Over time, this may become more popular as it will allow the publishers to provide access to the insights people want without exposing their full data collections. Some legal publishers have started to provide datasets by subscription, and this may be a common way to acquire access in the future.

2.3 Developing data

Where data is not available for a particular need, it is often still possible to develop or find data that will allow a project to move forward. There are many ways to do this, whether by developing systems that collect data or creating it manually. Two important ways to find data points for topics that do not have clear sources are through experiments and by finding proxies, or data points that are correlated with what is to be measured when it is not possible to measure the thing itself.

Experimental methodology

So far, the data sources listed in this chapter are for existing data arising from processes and documents that are already happening or which are already being created. Thinking beyond existing data, it is also possible to design experiments to develop data that does not exist to understand events and processed that have not happened yet. This allows researchers to understand possible outcomes under particular conditions in order to inform decision making. Experimental methods allow for better understanding of causation — as long as researchers are constrained to explore things that have happened, they can only confidently identify correlation. To identify causation, they need to know what the outcome would be if something different had happened. This is where good experimental design is crucial.

Experimental design in law can start with identifying techniques used in other disciplines and exploring new ways for them to be used. It may also require convincing decision makers to allow random assignment of categories among an experimental group. However, there are significant barriers to experimentation as a way to gather information about human subjects generally (Luca and Bazerman 2020, 64), and in law particularly (Lynch, Greiner, and

Cohen 2020). Jim Greiner of Harvard Access to Justice Lab has found that in law there is a strong "reliance on personal experience and lack of openness to the scientific process" in the legal sector (Neal 2020).

One important element of resolving objections to randomized testing is to explain why experiments are needed instead of simply implementing best practices for everyone. The answer is that often it is not clear what best practices are. In contrast, consider that in the current system, untested changes are made to the law for the whole population (Lynch, Greiner, and Cohen 2020). There will be limits to developing evidence based understanding of the legal system and policy until experimental methods are more widely adopted.

Proxy data

One of the first things to consider when developing a data strategy is that often the data to measure something directly is not available, so it may be necessary to find proxy data points correlated with what is to be measured instead. Proxy data is data about something that can be more easily measured, and which fluctuates, or is correlated, with the thing that cannot be measured directly.

One of the most common types of proxy data used in law firms is the recording of billable hours as a way to measure lawyer productivity: billable hours are not what makes a lawyer's contribution to a firm valuable. They are not directly connected to profitability because only time that gets billed and paid for generates revenue. Real contributions are not easy to count, as each lawyer's contribution gets combined in a single bill. Some of the time a lawyer worked may get written off and some bills may not get paid, which is not under a particular lawyer's control. Billable hours are even more remote from the value delivered to a client, as that is primarily a function of the quality of information received and process followed. These things are not easy to measure, but the number of hours worked is, so that is used as a measure of contribution.

The problem with using proxy data is that it frequently creates incentives to focus on maximizing the proxy instead of the underlying value. For example, in an environment where the primary metric for performance reviews for information technology staff is the number of help desk tickets resolved, they may be incentivized to create a large number of frivolous tickets that can be resolved quickly to the detriment of doing more valuable work. Once incentivized to do so, people may make significant changes to their behavior, which can reduce the value of the proxy by removing the link with the underlying value to be measured.

It is important to understand when a proxy is being used and how this affects outcomes. For example, in machine learning it is possible to extract information about which variables are most predictive of particular recommendations. However, just because a variable is the most predictive of a desired measure in a machine learning application does not mean it is a suitable proxy (Copus, Hübert, and Laqueur 2019, 56). This is where it is useful to consider the relationship between the correlated data and causation carefully.

2.4 Strategy

Developing a data strategy is necessary if effort and investment are not to be wasted. It is easy to start collecting large quantities of data from available sources without knowing what will be done with it, but these initiatives are often a misguided use of resources. Issues like deciding whether to collect and how to handle data that has not been adequately vetted for issues like privacy or client confidentiality should be considered early in the process: Cory Doctorow has gone so far as to call customer data "toxic waste" for the security issues it can entail (Doctorow 2020). Law firms in particular are generally sophisticated about managing client confidentiality, and these concerns should be addressed when new projects are developed and not as afterthoughts. There are significant costs associated with manually generating data, and it is imperative that the plan for design and future use be carefully considered before a project that requires this kind of effort is started.

Different types of data coming from multiple sources are suitable for particular applications. Here are some ways to plan and manage data collection:

- Manual data generation
- Narrowing the subject
- Crowdsourcing
- User generation
- Publicly available datasets
- Licensing third party data
- Collaboration with an organization with data
- Small acquisitions (Mueller-Freitag 2016)

Not all of these options will be suitable for all situations, but thinking creatively about how data can be acquired will allow for more sophisticated applications.

One important strategic consideration is who will manage a data program. Research looking at this question found that it is a mistake to ask an IT department to manage a data-driven team. IT teams are generally good at developing systems to store data and protect it, but they do not tend to excel at turning it into business value. (Jayasuriya 2018, 192–93).

2.5 Conclusion

There are many possible sources of data. Ready made data has the advantage of being less expensive, while custom data is more amenable to communicating exactly what is wanted. The two major emerging sources of data are increased government publication of their data and creation of data using experimental methods. With government data there will need to be political will to make it available and to solve problems like existing agreements with publishers that limit distribution, and resolve privacy concerns. The adoption of experimental methods in contrast is something that is within the ability of legal scholars and practitioners to fix. Looking to the future, there will almost certainly be new sources of data becoming available as well as emerging technologies that will make new methodologies possible. The next chapter will provide more detail about what kinds of data can be obtained from these sources.

Works cited

Ashley, Kevin D. 2017. *Artificial Intelligence and Legal Analytics: New Tools for Law Practice in the Digital Age*. Cambridge: Cambridge University Press.

Bailey, Jane, and Jacquelyn Burkell. 2017. "Revisiting the Open Court Principle in an Era of Online Publication: Questioning Presumptive Public Access to Parties' and Witnesses' Personal Information." *Ottawa Law Review* 48 (1): 143–181.

Carlson, Keith, Michael A. Livermore, and Daniel N. Rockmore. "The Problem of Data Bias in the Pool of Published U.S. Appellate Court Opinions." *Journal of Empirical Legal Studies* 17, no. 2 (2020): 224–261. https://doi.org/10.1111/jels.12253.

Copus, Ryan, Ryan Hübert, and Hannah Laqueur. 2019. "Big Data, Machine Learning, and the Credibility Revolution in Empirical Legal Studies." In *Law as Data: Computation, Text, and the Future of Legal Analysis*, 21–57. The SFI Press Seminar Series. Santa Fe: The SFI Press.

Doctorow, Cory. 2020. "Data: The New Oil, or Potential for a Toxic Oil Spill?" Secure Futures by Kaspersky. 2020. https://www.kaspersky.com/blog/secure-futures-maga zine/data-new-toxic-waste/34184/.

Eidelman, Vlad, Anastassia Kornilova, and Daniel Argyle. 2019. "Predicting Legislative Floor Action." In *Law as Data: Computation, Text, and the Future of Legal Analysis*, 117–150. The SFI Press Seminar Series. Santa Fe: The SFI Press.

Frug, Sara. 2021. (Co-Director at Legal Information Institute), in conversation with the author.

Grady, Kenneth A. 2018. "Mining Legal Data: Collecting and Analyzing 21st Century Gold." In *Data-Driven Law: Data Analytics and the New Legal Services*, edited by Edward Walters, 11–32. Boca Raton, FL: Auerbach Publications.

Hoadley, Daniel. "Open Access to Case Law – How Do We Get There?" Internet Newsletter for Lawyers (blog), November 23, 2018. https://www.infolaw.co.uk/news letter/2018/11/open-access-case-law-get/.

Hodgins, Kristin. 2021. Director of Legal Operations, Government of British Columbia, Canada, in discussion with the author.

Jayasuriya, Kumar. 2018. "Data Mining in the Law Firm: Using Internal Expertise to Drive Decision Making." In *Data-Driven Law: Data Analytics and the New Legal Services*, edited by Edward Walters, 189–198. Boca Raton, FL: Auerbach Publications.

Luca, Michael, and Max H.Bazerman. 2020. *The Power of Experiments: Decision Making in a Data-Driven World*. Cambridge, Massachusetts: The MIT Press.

Lynch, H. Fernandez, D. J. Greiner, and I. G. Cohen. 2020. "Overcoming Obstacles to Experiments in Legal Practice." *Science* 367 (6482): 1078–1080. https://doi.org/10.1126/science.aay3005.

Mobray, Andrew, and Philip Chung. 2021. (Co-Director and Executive Director AustLII [Australasian Legal Information Institute]), in discussion with the author.

Mueller-Freitag, Moritz. 2016. "10 Data Acquisition Strategies for Startups." *Medium.* May 31, 2016. https://medium.com/@muellerfreitag/10-data-acquisition-strategies-for-startups-47166580ee48.

Nayyer, Kim. 2021. (Edward Cornell Law Librarian, Associate Dean for Library Services, and Professor of the Practice at Cornell University), in discussion with the author.

Neal, Jeff. 2020. "Transforming Law into a Science." *Harvard Law Today.* November 10, 2020. https://today.law.harvard.edu/transforming-law-into-a-science/.

Salter, Shannon. 2021. (Chair at Civil Resolution Tribunal of British Columbia, and adjunct professor at the UBC Allard School of Law), in discussion with the author.

Treasury Board of Canada Secretariat. 2019. "Open by Default and Modern, Easy to Use Formats." Government of Canada Website. June 27, 2019. http://open.canada.ca/en/content/open-default-and-modern-easy-use-formats.

Winterton, Jules. 2021. (Chief Executive Officer, British and Irish Legal Information Institute (BAILII)), in discussion with the author.

Chapter 3

Data formats

3.1 Introduction

Data generally, and legal data specifically, come in many formats, but the majority of legal data is in the form of documents. Legal research in particular commonly uses documents in one of the following formats:

- Paper books or shorter documents
- PDF files that replicate paper formats including page numbers
- HTML webpages that provide text in a format that does not follow the format of a printed page
- XML files have more structure for computing, but which are typically presented as webpages indistinguishable from HTML files in user interfaces

These are formats that are designed for human users to access. There are also a wide range of computer readable formats, which are significantly simpler to analyze. It is much easier to present machine readable formats in user-friendly ways than it is to convert human centered display based formats to being machine readable.

This is because human centered formats primarily tend to have information encoded in them that are primarily focused on display, such as text alignment or font. Machine readable formats in contrast contain coding that is focused on the structure of the documents, which provides flexibility in how they can be displayed. Beyond textual documents, other data may be available in other various formats that encourage analysis, such as spreadsheets. It is generally easier to use data that is already created and available for use, though it will almost certainly need work to get it into usable formats. In contrast, developing a data collection plan for a particular project is generally more expensive, but the resulting data is often more ready for use.

3.2 Categories

Before discussing the complexities of data formats and how they affect the research it is possible to do, consider that even aggregating data about things

DOI: 10.4324/9781003127307-3

that seem simple can be quite difficult. Quantifying statistics can be complicated, and much of this has to do with how to define conditions and outcomes
into categories.

As an example, statisticians find it difficult to quantify relatively straightforward things like how many children die after heart surgery. This is partly due
to questions about defining the group to be studied:

- What age range constitutes children?
- What procedures count as heart surgery?
- How long after the surgery does a death stop being connected to the
  surgery?

It is also difficult to obtain tracking information about the individual patients;
what about children who were transferred to other hospitals (Spiegelhalter
2019, 19–21)? And these are basic statistics about an issue central to health
policy that is prioritized by society.

Researchers looking at issues like what proportions of cases are found in
favor of plaintiffs in personal injury claims have similar problems:

- How to account for plaintiffs who settle before or during trial?
- How do cases where there are multiple injuries get measured?
- What point in proceedings is counted as an outcome when there may be
  appeals, court costs, or other issues still to be resolved?

So, when developing a strategy, it is important to have working definitions for
things like what a "case" is for the purpose of analyzing effectiveness of a program.
Legal professionals and courts tend to think of a "case" as an individual matter
dealing with a particular set of facts and area of law that would be handled dis-
cretely from other matters and generally measure it that way. In this paradigm, an
individual's criminal and family law matters would be separated. In contrast, litigants may not see these issues as separate: individuals interacting with the justice
system tend to think of all interactions with the court system as one experience, so
criminal, family law, landlord and tenant, and employment proceedings may all
affect perceptions of each other (Sutherland 2013). Deciding what makes the most
sense as a frame is a necessary component of the process.

This lack of shared definitions of elements in the legal environment also
extends to outcomes. Contrary to the expectations created by Hollywood
movies, where so many lawyers have "never lost a case", legal outcomes are
complex and can be considered wins or losses depending on context. It is difficult to evaluate the effectiveness of interventions when situations and outcomes
are so varied (Sutherland 2013). For traditional legal research this does not tend
to matter, because outlying cases with extreme outcomes define a range of likely
results which lawyers evaluate with their judgment making predictions on
where in the range a particular matter is likely to fall. There are several legal

research tools that are based on this principle especially for sentencing and personal injury awards, but they rely on human judgement to make predictions on what is likely in any particular situation. Statistical analysis in particular requires considerable certainty about the kinds of data that are included and their distribution, so defining the categories and assigning them correctly is imperative for reliable conclusions.

3.3 Issues particular to law

There are many issues particular to accessing the primary law as data in particular, and any use of these sources as datasets will be easier if they are addressed.

Case citations

Having standardized, open standards for citation of legal documents, particularly court and tribunal decisions, is a significant benefit for the use of law as data where it is present and a hinderance where it is not. Canada has had a neutral citation standard since the early 2000s, which allows anyone who needs access to case law to find it regardless of where they access it. In contrast, in the United States many courts require that commercial citations to print volumes be used, so justice system participants are required to wait for the books to be published before they can finalize the citation information in their systems (Arredondo 2021). In Africa, there is no shared citation system and in many cases there is no jurisdiction information in citations, especially for historical documents, which significantly limits the ability to correctly attribute documents to particular countries (du Toit 2021). These issues are relevant around the world and spending time to understand citation practices will help make a project successful.

Depth of data

Legal documents tend to be relatively few in number but long in length. This is referred to as deep data, where individual documents have significant content and depth, which contains more detail than the number of documents to be analyzed does. This is atypical of datasets in most sectors, and most available techniques do not make good use of the depth available in legal documents like court decisions (Soh 2021). Machine learning tends to be more affective with this kind of data than traditional statistical techniques. See Section 4.3 for further discussion of this issue.

Machine readable law

There is a great deal of research being done into ways to integrate primary law more effectively into computer applications — one side of this is making applications that can parse law, and the other is developing formats for publishing the law that will better facilitate these uses across applications. Governments tend to view consumers of law as individuals who read and access it one document at a time, which can lead to situations where agencies publish documents as image PDFs and consider this as making it digitally available. It may be true that for consumers of law who are individuals reading single documents without the need for assistive technology to access it, this may be sufficient, but if the consumer of law is viewed as the public as a whole this is a failure (Walters 2021).

One important element of creating documents that are useful as data is formatting them in ways that support the ways they will be used, and some formats support more uses than others. The classic format that laws have been published in is print with formal formatting elements that vary by institution, whether by originating body or publisher. There have been some efforts internationally to develop standards for elements to be included, but it is an ongoing struggle to ensure necessary elements are included (Winterton 2021). When these documents started being published electronically, this format was mirrored when the documents were published in PDF. PDF is a good display format, and it prints well, which allows documents to be presented in ways that imitate paper copies, but it provides limited functionality outside of those uses.

PDF is not the best option for uses like information retrieval, while HTML and XML provide better functionality for those applications. If it is required to edit legislation, such as inserting amended sections, then sections and paragraphs need to be marked and more specialized, dynamic formats like Akoma Ntoso (Cervone, Palmirani, and Vitali n.d.) or LegalDocML (Palmirani and Vitali 2020) are more useful. If instead the goal is to have computer applications that can start to reason about the law and what is permitted, then none of these formats is sufficient. To do this, documents would need to be written in languages designed to hold this kind of semantic information. The concepts around this kind of coding language have roots going back to research that started in the 1980s, but there is presently a renewed push to develop the coding languages that will support this kind of application (Morris 2021).

3.4 Types

There are several different types of data that can be used for analysis. At a high level, these include numerical, categorical, and textual data. Each of these can convey different information.

Numerical

Numerical data can be expressed by integers on a number line. It is the most common and usable data type for statistical analysis in many sectors, but in many cases, it is not available for questions that arise in legal contexts because it has not been a priority to collect it. This is partly because many legal situations and outcomes do not lend themselves well to being counted. This is in contrast with scientific disciplines like medicine that have generated extensive quantitative numerical data and integrated it into their practices for many years.

Numerical data can describe many things. It may also come in different file formats, but tables and spreadsheets are common ways to convey a series of values. Common types of data that may be available for use in legal research include:

- Financial information
- Data about participation in the legal system
- Lengths of sentences
- Quanta for damages

Where numerical data does not exist, researchers may be required to compile it themselves. This is often done through manual transcription or programmatic parsing of text in documents to pull out the values.

Categorical

Categorical data may look like numerical data because it is often signified by numerals, but the characters in these datasets signify that entries are to be grouped in categories. The values of the numerals, or whatever characters are used, are not significant. These categories can be binary with each category designated by a numeral or letter (0,1, a,b, and y,n are common choices), but there is theoretically no limit to the number of categories that can be evaluated. That said, it is quite possible to run into the practical limit of the upper bound of what particular software packages and computer set ups can handle. Some examples of categorical data include:

- How a defendant pled in court
- Whether costs awards were awarded
- What practice group manages the file for a particular client
- Whether a party is represented by a lawyer

Categorical data can give complex analyses when used well, for example they can show relationships that may not be otherwise apparent by simplifying data so that it can be compared more easily. This is especially useful in conjunction with other data types as a way to divide datasets into smaller samples with particular attributes that can then be analyzed separately.

Free text

Free text data is the most common data type available in law. Free text simply means that this type of data is made up of natural language. Common sources of free text data in law include:

- Case law
- Legislation
- Internal documents such as emails and memos
- Government documents

These can be analyzed as text using techniques like machine learning, or they can be modified using techniques to extract numerical or categorical data before they are analyzed.

Common examples of numerical or categorical information that can be pulled from free text are time ranges and monetary values. Free text data can also be used as a source for tools that analyze the language itself allowing for extraction of information about topics such as:

- How different writers discuss different subjects
- Topic identification
- Automatic summarization of texts

The practical and technological limits on analyzing large bodies of text have been some of the major barriers to the use of data methods in law. As computing power grows and techniques are perfected and brought in from other disciplines, this is becoming less of an issue. Legal scholars and practitioners are increasingly able to bring in best practices others have developed and move forward quickly.

3.5 Delivery formats

For each of the types of data listed above, there are many possible delivery formats. The easiest types of data to handle are those that are already in a computer readable format. These are usually tagged formats like CSV, JSON, and XML. It frequently does not matter which of these formats the data is in, because they can relatively easily be converted from one to another. Figure 3.1 shows an example of JSON formatted data related to bills from United States Congress.

Open data activists call for governments to make their data available in these kinds of formats because they are most easily used without substantial work needed to prepare them. Because so much legal data is comprised of documents, document first formats like PDF or DOCX are also common. These require more processing to prepare them for use than tagged data formats do. Even where electronic versions of documents are available, they may not be in tagged formats. HTML is a common format used on websites. It has tags which may make it look like tagged data, but HTML tags control display, they do not typically mark parts of documents or convey as much about structure and meaning.

Instead of fully tagged or plain text, legal information tends to be distributed in semi-structured formats. This means that they frequently have titles and some fields labeled in the document, but that these are not controlled in a

```
 1  {
 2      "status": "OK",
 3      "copyright": "Copyright (c) 2017 Pro Publica Inc. All Rights Reserved.",
 4      "results": [{
 5          "congress": 115,
 6          "chamber": "House",
 7          "num_results": 20,
 8          "offset": 0,
 9          "bills": [{
10              "bill_id": "hr4256-115",
11              "bill_slug": "hr4256",
12              "bill_type": "hr",
13              "number": "H.R.4256",
14              "bill_uri": "https://api.propublica.org/congress/v1/115/bills/hr4256.json",
15              "title": "To amend the Public Health Service Act to authorize the expansion of activities
                    related to Alzheimer's disease, cognitive decline, and brain health under the Alzheimer's
                    Disease and Healthy Aging Program, and for other purposes.",
16              "short_title": "To amend the Public Health Service Act to authorize the expansion of
                    activities related to Alzheimer's disease, cognitive decline, and brain health under the
                    Alzheimer's Disease and Healthy Aging Program, and for other purposes.",
17              "sponsor_title": "Rep.",
18              "sponsor_id": "G000558",
19              "sponsor_name": "Brett Guthrie",
20              "sponsor_state": "KY",
21              "sponsor_party": "R",
22              "sponsor_uri": "https://api.propublica.org/congress/v1/members/G000558.json",
23              "gpo_pdf_uri": null,
24              "congressdotgov_url": "https://www.congress.gov/bill/115th-congress/house-bill/4256",
25              "govtrack_url": "https://www.govtrack.us/congress/bills/115/hr4256",
26              "introduced_date": "2017-11-06",
27              "active": false,
28              "last_vote": null,
29              "house_passage": null,
30              "senate_passage": null,
31              "enacted": null,
32              "vetoed": null,
33              "cosponsors": 3,
34              "cosponsors_by_party": {
35                  "D": 2,
36                  "R": 1
37              },
38              "committees": "House Energy and Commerce Committee",
39              "committee_codes": ["HSIF"],
40              "subcommittee_codes": [],
41              "primary_subject": "",
42              "summary": "",
```

Figure 3.1 A JSON file with United States Congress bill data. Available on the ProPublica Congress API.

systematic way for all fields that may be needed to identify the parts of the document that are of interest. This makes it difficult to extract outcomes without manual examination of the text and significant data processing before it can be used. Some information can be extracted using automated algorithms or techniques like regular expressions, but these require a set of standard documents be available to work from.

This is not always readily available for the kinds of issues most relevant to understanding the social impact of the justice system. As was discussed in Chapter 2, written judgements are often not published for routine matters and beyond that, data may not be being collected at all. If data does start getting collected for a particular project, the process can be designed according to best practices. The coming sections will discuss certain format considerations for assessing available data and designing what data collection processes will be used.

Michael Lissner of the Free Law Project has found that different types of organizations and individuals request access to primary law data in different formats: organizations that provide ongoing information services such as bank due diligence request access to a search API, whereas start-ups frequently want a full bulk data export that replicates the entire database. Researchers tend to want zip files that give a snapshot of the dataset at a particular moment in time (Lissner 2021). Whether specific data formats such as those listed here will be available for any particular dataset varies by jurisdiction and institution, so local verification will be needed.

Spreadsheets

Spreadsheets can include any of the three primary types of data as different values can be put into spreadsheet cells. In addition to static data, spreadsheet programs also include the ability to generate new values for numerical fields through the use of formulae. Common spreadsheet file types include xls, csv, tsv, and xlsx. They can be opened in software like Microsoft Excel, Apple Pages, or Google Sheets. The advantage of csv files in particular is that there is no coding attached with the values, so they are flexible and can be opened in many software packages including text editors such as WordPad, TextEdit, or Sublime Text. This makes them more flexible, but they will not store formulae, so if that is required a different file type will be needed instead.

Tagged formats

Unlike spreadsheets which are displayed in columns and rows, tagged data formats display vertically down the screen or page if printed. These include common formats such as:

- XML
- JSON

They use conventions using uncommon punctuation to designate categories for the different data points, and what parts of the files correspond to those categories. See Figure 3.2 for an example of how data looks in XML.

These formats have many advantages:

- They are flexible, as categories can be defined based on a particular dataset
- They are designed for use in computer applications, so they can be leveraged in creative ways
- They can often easily be converted into other formats as needed

Many people working in the legal technology space hope that as time passes these computer friendly formats will become more prevalent, especially in the publication of primary law. This will allow for more development of dynamic uses for this data.

```
 1   <?xml version="1.0" encoding="UTF-8"?>
 2   <ActsRegsList>
 3   <Acts>
 4   <Act>
 5   <UniqueId>A-1</UniqueId>
 6   <OfficialNumber>A-1</OfficialNumber>
 7   <Language>eng</Language>
 8   <LinkToXML>http://laws-lois.justice.gc.ca/eng/XML/A-1.xml</LinkToXML>
 9   <LinkToHTMLToC>http://laws-lois.justice.gc.ca/eng/acts/A-1/index.html</LinkToHTMLToC>
10   <Title>Access to Information Act</Title>
11   <CurrentToDate>2021-06-03</CurrentToDate>
12   <RegsMadeUnderAct><Reg idRef="638933e"/><Reg idRef="638953e"/><Reg idRef="878430e"/><Reg
     idRef="896956e"/><Reg idRef="918831e"/></RegsMadeUnderAct>
13   </Act>
14   <Act>
15   <UniqueId>A-1</UniqueId>
16   <OfficialNumber>A-1</OfficialNumber>
17   <Language>fra</Language>
18   <LinkToXML>http://laws-lois.justice.gc.ca/fra/XML/A-1.xml</LinkToXML>
19   <LinkToHTMLToC>http://laws-lois.justice.gc.ca/fra/lois/A-1/index.html</LinkToHTMLToC>
20   <Title>Loi sur l'accès à l'information</Title>
21   <CurrentToDate>2021-06-03</CurrentToDate>
22   <RegsMadeUnderAct><Reg idRef="627530f"/><Reg idRef="627550f"/><Reg idRef="866777f"/><Reg
     idRef="885277f"/><Reg idRef="907152f"/></RegsMadeUnderAct>
23   </Act>
24   <Act>
25   <UniqueId>A-0.6</UniqueId>
26   <OfficialNumber>2019, c. 10</OfficialNumber>
27   <Language>eng</Language>
28   <LinkToXML>http://laws-lois.justice.gc.ca/eng/XML/A-0.6.xml</LinkToXML>
29   <LinkToHTMLToC>http://laws-lois.justice.gc.ca/eng/acts/A-0.6/index.html</LinkToHTMLToC>
30   <Title>Accessible Canada Act</Title>
31   <CurrentToDate>2021-06-03</CurrentToDate>
32   <RegsMadeUnderAct><Reg idRef="1190628e"/></RegsMadeUnderAct>
33   </Act>
34   <Act>
35   <UniqueId>A-0.6</UniqueId>
36   <OfficialNumber>2019, ch. 10</OfficialNumber>
37   <Language>fra</Language>
38   <LinkToXML>http://laws-lois.justice.gc.ca/fra/XML/A-0.6.xml</LinkToXML>
39   <LinkToHTMLToC>http://laws-lois.justice.gc.ca/fra/lois/A-0.6/index.html</LinkToHTMLToC>
40   <Title>Loi canadienne sur l'accessibilité</Title>
41   <CurrentToDate>2021-06-03</CurrentToDate>
42   <RegsMadeUnderAct><Reg idRef="1176810f"/></RegsMadeUnderAct>
43   </Act>
44   <Act>
```

Figure 3.2 An XML file with Canadian legislative data. Available on the Open Government Portal under the Canada Open Government Licence.

Databases

Databases are organized groupings of data that can be searched or accessed electronically. Databases can be accessed through a user facing interface like many online research tools' search interfaces, or programmatically through a back end interface that is designed for computers to use. Databases have the advantage of being easy to scale, so they can handle large volumes of data in an easy to access way. Databases are commonly used in libraries and research products, such as primary law and article collections.

APIs

API is short for "application programming interface", and they provide a way for computer applications to query databases programmatically without having to use the user facing interface. Many organizations have them, and they have become the basis for many kinds of business functions. These can include capabilities like the ability to embed maps into other websites or allowing users to make reservations on a restaurant's website through a third-party service.

In law, they have been less widely adopted than in other sectors for many reasons. Firstly, many legal organizations treat their data assets as sources of competitive advantage, and they may not want to share access to them, or there may be restrictions on what they can do with the data. There has also been a lack of investment in computing resources in law by governments in many jurisdictions, which are the ultimate source of primary law data. The last reason is that many developers are not interested in developing on top of other systems and would prefer to have full copies of data locally.

At the time of writing, the most frequent request on social media is for full downloads of datasets so that they can be analyzed as opposed to dynamic access through APIs. That said, APIs are good ways to provide resources for others to build useful tools. Going forward, they may be more widely adopted in law as more data savvy people explore the law and see more uses for them.

3.6 Considerations

There are many things to consider when assessing what methodology to use for available data.

Data standards

The lack of standardized formats for legal documents is a significant limitation for publication and use of data. The lack of standardized citation formats, or requirements to cite to particular commercial publications is one limit that was discussed in Section 3.3. There are also concerns such as legal documents that incorporate images which are not in accessible formats. This can include things like maps or technical drawings, but also images of data tables or other partially textual information. These, and other artifacts of historical practices, mean that it can be difficult to present documents in ways that can be easily used for data extraction, enable access by accessibility devices, or even support basic web navigation. Beyond this, there are also situations where documents like technical standards, which may be copyrighted, are integrated into regulations through a mechanism referred to as incorporation by reference (Frug 2021).

Passively and actively collected data

While it is not necessarily an aspect of format, it is important to know that data may be passively or actively collected. Passively collected data can be collected as a by product of other work, such as website usage statistics or data collected in law firms' practice management systems. Actively collected data is data that is intentionally collected as a primary activity. This includes activities like surveys, manually recording observations of behavior, and tracking user activity on a website. Actively collected or purposefully generated data can be designed so that it is in a format that can be easily used for diverse or particular purposes.

Passively collected data is more often available than actively collected data, and it may require more work to prepare it before it is usable. It is also generally significantly cheaper than actively collected data, because there is less investment needed in human and computing resources, because it is a byproduct of another activity that is already happening. That said, it may have issues because the systems collecting it are typically not designed for whatever purpose the data will be used for, which means that it may be more likely to push researchers to make tradeoffs with quality. These tradeoffs should be made consciously and can include things like inclusion of bias from existing behavior, which should be taken into account.

Large sets of passively collected data are becoming available but closer analyses of them often show biases in the processes used to generate them, and close attention needs to be paid to these issues if passively collected datasets are to be relied on (Pechenick, Danforth, and Dodds 2015). It may also necessitate the use of proxies, which are data points that are correlated with the thing to be measured where the thing itself cannot be measured directly. Proxy data is used when researchers want to research something and desired data points are not available or not easily measurable. It is important to remember that the use of proxies may lessen the connection with the underlying values (see Section 2.3 for more on proxy data).

Active data collection provides more control as processes are purposely designed, but thought still needs to be given to ensuring that what is collected can convey what researchers want to know. These new research tools can give insights that were impossible before, but this must be tempered with realistic understanding of possible biases in the data (Carlson, Livermore, and Rockmore 2020) even where best practices have been followed in systems' design.

This distinction between passively and actively collected data can illustrate issues associated with the use of artificial intelligence in law: there is a difference between data driven and symbolic approaches to artificial intelligence. Data driven approaches develop plans based on what is available and move forward from there, while symbolic driven approaches ensure there is understanding of what the data symbolizes and analyzes that instead. Investing in the time required for real knowledge acquisition tasks that yield accurate and explainable tools (Atkinson 2020).

Supervised and unsupervised machine learning

The difference between supervised and unsupervised machine learning is discussed elsewhere in this book, especially in Section 4.4, but there are important format considerations before either can be attempted.

Supervised machine learning provides outputs that can be explained more easily. However, it requires labeled data. Labeled data is data that has defined fields for things like author and time periods, and it can be in many formats including CSV, JSON, XML, and database formats. The main advantage is that these labels mean that it is easy to explain what elements of the dataset machine learning recommendations are based on. This is especially important in law as there are frequently prescribed criteria can be used when making particular decisions, such as prohibited grounds of discrimination, rules about the use of unrelated evidence, and restrictions on what evidence can entered at court.

Unfortunately, it is generally not possible to scale labeled data to large datasets, because creating it is too labor intensive, so in many cases unlabeled data is used for unsupervised machine learning instead. Unsupervised learning does not require the manual assignment of labels to datasets to run, which makes it significantly cheaper and more scalable. Unsupervised methods that are used on text alone do not typically give results that can be explained.

Researchers are working toward approaches that are explicable, while minimizing manual intervention, which will be necessary for the widespread adoption of applications like case prediction (Ferro et al. 2019, 12). Predicting court outcomes is one of the foci for machine learning research in law, and it requires adequate data inputs, which usually need to be labeled. As an example, when Daniel Katz, Michael Bommarito II, and Josh Blackman, created their system for predicting Supreme Court of the United States cases in the mid-2010s, they used data from the Supreme Court Database, which includes more than 200 years of quality, expertly coded data on court outcomes for the Supreme Court of the United States (Katz, Bommarito, II, and Blackman 2017). The database has up to 240 variables for each case including chronology, case background, judge, and outcome variables (Washington University Law n.d.). Without preexisting databases such as this, it can be prohibitively expensive and difficult to run supervised machine learning.

Law as code and law as data

There have been suggestions that in the future laws should shift toward being written as executable code in a programming language as that would take some of the ambiguity out of governance (Frankenreiter and Livermore 2019, 3). It is important to make the distinction between law as code and law as data. In recent years many researchers and developers in the legal space have been calling for laws to be presented as code. They argue this would allow better automated enforcement of the law and increase efficiency in the legal system.

To understand the distinction between law as code and law as data, it may help to visualize law as code as being exemplified by tax completion software. Each rule from the tax laws is programed into the software, and they are executed as information is added. Governments could choose to design and pass laws this way, and it could remove ambiguity from the legislation. This is different from law as data, where existing or new laws are parsed as data with conclusions drawn based on the laws in human readable language as they are published now. Though there would not be a barrier to treating law both as code and as a data source.

Law as code would require significant changes to the formats of legal documents, including things like limiting what types of information can be included and possibly expressing their substance in computer executable language which could then be converted into a more human friendly format for reading. By necessity, laws expressed in human language contain ambiguity through their syntax, but computer code does not have this constraint (Ashley 2017, 45).

However, ambiguity in laws, especially statutes, may be a feature that serves valid purposes. It may be that legislators have no desire to remove it, rather they may prefer to leave room for courts to interpret their words to consider the detail of each individual case (Ashley 2017, 40). This is semantic ambiguity, which allows for the application of human expertise, meaning that laws do not have to consider every possible situation in advance. Semantic ambiguity may also be left in legislation when it is not politically feasible to agree to the finer details of how a law will be implemented. Maintaining this kind of politically expedient ambiguity in laws is not inappropriate as it helps governments operate more smoothly. In contrast, syntactic ambiguity results from imprecision in language, which can be inevitable, as human language is by definition imprecise, or it can be the result of carelessness if, for example, terms are now properly defined. Semantic ambiguity may be useful but syntactic ambiguity has no utility (Morris 2021). See Chapter 6.4 for further discussion of ambiguity in the context of law.

3.7 Planning

When deciding on a plan for creating and storing data, it is important to consider how it will be used, continue to be robust, and deliver value over time. This should be part of the wider decisions surrounding strategy. It is difficult to anticipate how data will be used in the future, but certain planned steps can make it easier. For example, collected data should be stored with tags connecting it with the source, especially if it is associated with law firms' clients. Otherwise there is the risk that whole databases will need to be deleted when records associated with a particular client cannot be extracted (Grady 2018, 28).

It is also prudent to remember that analyses cannot normally be extrapolated into the future beyond the timeframe covered in the original analysis. When this is desired, care will have to be taken that systems accept new data in deliberate ways and that they will be updated and tested before they go live. Live systems should not be constantly updating with new data without being verified before they are used for real world applications, as this increases the risk of unintended consequences (Chatila 2020). It is also recommended to consider that legal data publishing changes regularly and speaking with stakeholders at agencies and publishers who make this content available is prudent to try to integrate these changes into plans as early as possible.

Effective planning for data formats can have significant benefits. When Singaporean case law started being published online, extensive work was put into ensuring that the format was robust, and that it was designed to be used in different ways into the future with good coding defining the parts of documents, so that it could be used dynamically (Soh 2021). This means that research is easier to carry out using that data than it is in many other jurisdictions.

3.8 Conclusion

Understanding the formatting issues associated with the data to be used will significantly increase the likelihood of success in any data driven project. Where data comes from, how it was gathered, and how it is recorded and presented, all make differences in how it can be used and what conclusions can be drawn from it. In any project dealing with legal data, make sure to consider the long timelines in legal organizations. Decisions may have repercussions far into the future: public acts in the United Kingdom were required to be printed on vellum as archival copies until 2015. Now they are printed in archival paper (Kelly 2018). These timelines also need to account for responsibilities to posterity. The law needs to continue to be available indefinitely, and in some places this is more difficult than others. In the Pacific Islands for example, humidity is so high that print copies degrade quickly making electronic versions more stable (Mobray and Chung 2021). Over time, new formats will develop, and emerging techniques may make untagged data more usable, but these considerations will continue to be important in any data driven endeavor. The next chapter will discuss techniques for how legal data can be used.

Works cited

Arredondo, Pablo. 2021. (Co-Founder and Chief Product Officer at Casetext), in conversation with the author.

Ashley, Kevin D. 2017. *Artificial Intelligence and Legal Analytics: New Tools for Law Practice in the Digital Age*. Cambridge: Cambridge University Press.

Atkinson, Katie. 2020. "Explainability for AI and Law in the Wild." Presented at the JURIX 2020: 33rd International Conference on Legal Knowledge and Information Systems, Virtual, December 10.

Carlson, Keith, Michael A. Livermore, and Daniel N. Rockmore. 2020. "The Problem of Data Bias in the Pool of Published U.S. Appellate Court Opinions." *Journal of Empirical Legal Studies* 17 (2): 224–261. https://doi.org/10.1111/jels.12253.

Cervone, Luca, Monica Palmirani, and Fabio Vitali. n.d. "*Akoma Ntoso*." Akoma Ntoso Site. Accessed June 6, 2021. http://www.akomantoso.org/.

Chatila, Raja. 2020. "*Can AI Systems Be Trustworthy?*" Presented at the JURIX 2020: 33rd International Conference on Legal Knowledge and Information Systems, Virtual, December 11.

Ferro, Lisa, John Aberdeen, Karl Branting, Craig Pfeifer, Alexander Yeh, and Amartya Chakraborty. 2019. "Scalable Methods for Annotating Legal-Decision Corpora." In *Proceedings of the Natural Legal Language Processing Workshop 2019*, 12–20. Minneapolis, Minnesota: Association for Computational Linguistics. https://www.aclweb.org/anthology/W19-22.pdf.

Frankenreiter, Jens, and Michael A. Livermore. 2019. "Computational Methods in Legal Analysis." SSRN Scholarly Paper ID 3568558. Rochester, NY: Social Science Research Network. https://papers.ssrn.com/abstract=3568558.

Frug, Sara. 2021. (Co-Director at Legal Information Institute), in conversation with the author.

Grady, Kenneth A. 2018. "Mining Legal Data: Collecting and Analyzing 21st Century Gold." In *Data-Driven Law: Data Analytics and the New Legal Services*, edited by Edward Walters, 11–32. Boca Raton, FL: Auerbach Publications.

Katz, Daniel Martin, Michael J. Bommarito, II, and Josh Blackman. 2017. "A General Approach for Predicting the Behavior of the Supreme Court of the United States." *PLOS ONE* 12 (4): e0174698. https://doi.org/10.1371/journal.pone.0174698.

Kelly, Richard. 2018. "Vellum: Printing Record Copies of Public Acts." Research Briefing. UK Parliament. https://commonslibrary.parliament.uk/research-briefings/cbp-7451/.

Lissner, Michael. 2021. (Executive Director at Free Law Project), in discussion with the author.

Mobray, Andrew, and Philip Chung. 2021. (Co-Director and Executive Director AustLII [Australasian Legal Information Institute]), in discussion with the author.

Morris, Jason. 2021. (Principal Research Engineer, Symbolic Artificial Intelligence for the Singapore Management University Centre for Computational Law), in discussion with the author.

Palmirani, Monica, and Fabio Vitali. 2020. "OASIS LegalDocumentML (LegalDocML) TC." Oasis Open. 2020. https://www.oasis-open.org/committees/tc_home.php?wg_abbrev=legaldocml.

Pechenick, Eitan Adam, Christopher M. Danforth, and Peter Sheridan Dodds. 2015. "Characterizing the Google Books Corpus: Strong Limits to Inferences of Socio-Cultural and Linguistic Evolution." *PLOS ONE* 10 (10): e0137041. https://doi.org/10.1371/journal.pone.0137041.

ProPublica. n.d. "Bills — ProPublica Congress API." ProPublica Website. Accessed July 4, 2021. https://projects.propublica.org/api-docs/congress-api/bills/.

Soh, Jerrold. 2021. (Assistant Professor of Law and Deputy Director, Centre for Computational Law at the Singapore Management University), in discussion with the author.

Spiegelhalter, David. 2019. *The Art of Statistics: Learning from Data.* New York: Viking.

Sutherland, Sarah. 2013. "Using Data to Leverage Access to Justice." *Slaw* (blog). August 1, 2013. http://www.slaw.ca/2013/08/01/using-data-to-leverage-access-to-justice/.

Toit, Neil du. 2021. (AfricanLII Data Scientist, University of Cape Town), in conversation with the author.

Walters, Ed. 2021. (CEO at Fastcase), in discussion with the author.

Washington University Law. n.d. "The Supreme Court Database." Accessed August 2, 2020. http://scdb.wustl.edu/.

Winterton, Jules. 2021. (Chief Executive Officer, British and Irish Legal Information Institute (BAILII)), in discussion with the author.

Chapter 4

Data analysis techniques

4.1 Introduction

A full review of the topic of data analysis techniques is beyond the scope of this book. However, understanding some of what is possible and what holds promise for further research helps show ways to move forward. Furthermore, new techniques do not come from a vacuum but are rather built on what currently exists, so understanding these topics can also help give a mental framework for emerging ways to understand the law into the future as well as in the present.

One issue to understand is that the computing tools used with legal data were primarily developed in other fields, and researchers have not exhausted what any of them can say about the law in particular and legal data in general. Many of these techniques come from primary research in computer science, especially research into natural language processing.

Research developments generally follow a regular cycle from development to widespread adoption, and this process generally takes twenty years or more to make the full transition from primary research to community facing deployment. Here is a general flow of how primary research is integrated into law:

- Development as primary research by computer scientists
- Adoption by other fields where techniques are further developed
- Research by legal scholars and developers into what they can use from these techniques
- Maturation of these tools as research generating techniques in law progresses
- Exploration of the potential of this technique for commercial purposes through research and development
- Launch of practice or public facing tools using the technology
- Integration of the technology into people's interactions with the law

Generally, research into the law has not been one of the first novel applications these techniques have been used for as they are developed. This has many causes, such as:

DOI: 10.4324/9781003127307-4

- The intractability of legal source material
- Conservatism in the culture of law
- Lack of access to appropriate sources of data
- Relative low interest in pursuing this work

This may change going forward as more researchers become comfortable with exploring the potential for computational techniques to drive valuable insights and as more interdisciplinary relationships are formed. However, it takes years or decades for technological change to become widespread in situations where there is significant educational and financial investment required to implement it (Underwood 2019, 161).

That said, computing techniques are becoming better able to manage large amounts of complicated text, and this will create new opportunities. Old computational techniques did not allow for the range of outcomes that reflect reality. For example, results were often presented in binary options. New tools allow for more variety and nuance with "almost no limits on the scale of the representation." (Dumas and Frankenreiter 2019, 61) This increased sophistication means that it is possible to see how these tools can move from curiosities into productive use when dealing with datasets as complex as legal documents.

There is a range of computational tools available for analyzing text, and they range from relatively simple to complex. Simple tools might look at analyzing numerical attributes such as the relative length of court decisions or language attributes such as word use or sentence length. This may also include applications like network analysis of citation patterns. As they become more complex, natural language processing and other methodologies are now making it possible to also do more ambitious analyses. Commonly used techniques include bag-of-words approaches which look at word occurrence, and word vector analyses which provide deeper understanding of meaning.

As time goes on, more complex tools will be developed and used, driven by the improvement of the technology, reductions in cost of computing, and increase in availability of software set up to run analyses that will reduce the need for researchers to have sophisticated coding knowledge themselves.

4.2 Close reading

It may seem odd to include close reading in a chapter on data analysis techniques, but it is a technique worth considering for several reasons. In a field that draws so significantly on interpreting the detail of words and writers' intentions, close reading is, and will continue to be, an important component of legal practice and scholarship. Computing tools provide insights that close reading cannot — they bring the ability to examine a breadth of content and identify details of patterns that humans miss. However, gaining insight into human beings' words, discerning the social and cultural importance of the law, and understanding how it affects human lives will continue to be best assessed by human readers.

Close reading as a technique is not broken or outdated. It continues to work as it has for millennia. But now that other tools are available, they show the gaps in what close reading can do: "Although this method has supported centuries of scholarship. It is also limiting, both in terms of the amount of data that can be processed, and in terms of the types of analysis that are possible." (Frankenreiter and Livermore 2019, 1)

Considerable legal education is devoted to teaching law students to read like lawyers and how to extract details of the law from the narrative format of court judgements (Livermore and Rockmore 2019, 6), but there have been calls to improve the interpretation of law using mathematical methods for a long time. In 1897 Oliver Wendell Homes Jr. said: "For the rational study of the law the blackletter man may be the man of the present, but the man of the future is the man of statistics and the master of economics." (Holmes, Jr. 1897) Whether this will hold to be true remains to be seen, but the best hope seems to be that over time human skills and insight will integrate information from computing techniques, and this will enhance both.

4.3 Statistical analysis

Statistical techniques can be used as tools to understand diverse topics such as legal documents, actors in the legal process, and the causes and outcomes of laws and their implementation. There is great variety in possible analyses that can be done with statistics, though there are also significant limitations deriving from the availability of appropriate data and the structure of existing data. Many of these strategies fall under the umbrella of data mining, which aims to find patterns in data.

Most statistical analysis relies on numerical data, which can be especially difficult to acquire in law. Researchers may be able to get access to well prepared research data, such as The Supreme Court Database published by Washington University Law (Washington University Law n.d.), which provides detailed data about many attributes of cases from the United States Supreme Court. However, for most topics there will be more work required to acquire and prepare legal data than researchers anticipate, and in many cases researchers will have to compile it themselves. This is especially problematic for researchers who want to perform social science research related to law, because legal documents are an incomplete record of individuals' lived experiences with legal problems and interactions with the justice system. This is discussed in more detail in Chapter 3.

The first step in deciding how to evaluate data is to look at its structure and source. For simple numerical data this is usually done by graphing it and looking for patterns, but for more complex datasets this will be more complicated as it becomes difficult for human eyes to discern overly complex patterns. In datasets there are many possible distribution patterns. Some of the most common include the following:

Normal distribution

Normal distribution is a common pattern in many populations described using numerical data, such as human height. This pattern is exemplified by a small number of outliers at each end and a majority of results in the middle, creating a classic hump shape. Some examples of where normal distributions would be expected to be encountered in law include sentence lengths and financial awards.

Random distribution

Data may also have a simple random distribution with no pattern. This could mean that the attributes being graphed are not correlated, or the appearance of randomness could mask a pattern that is not apparent. This situation may require further exploration to see if patterns become apparent with different parameters, but it is important to avoid repeatedly analyzing or resampling data as it is possible to identify patterns artificially that do not appear in the data as a whole when doing this.

Linear distribution

Data may have a linear pattern. Common possibilities for linear patterns include straight lines, parabolas, broken lines where values jump at a certain point, and irregular curves. It is also possible that the pattern may be ambiguous. In these cases it becomes a judgement call which shape best fits the data.

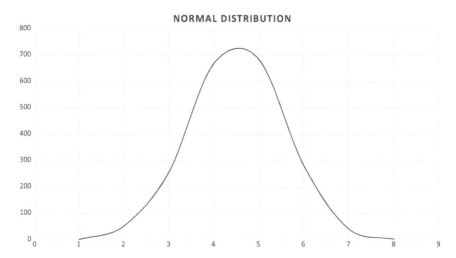

Figure 4.1 A sample normal distribution

Multiple points of comparison

When looking at more complex datasets it is common to have multiple numerical values for each entry. In this case it may be worth comparing each against the other to see which have patterns. Figure 4.2 includes an example of this type of comparison.

Techniques

Statistical techniques enable researchers to look for patterns in source data. Here are two common possible tools:

T-tests

T-tests are mathematical assessments that can be used to identify and compare averages for data that follow a normal distribution. An example where this could be used in a legal context could be to compare the range of sentences for two groups of people who may be treated differently because of inappropriate criteria such as race or gender. This is important because it can identify patterns in the data that may not be apparent because the data points overlap.

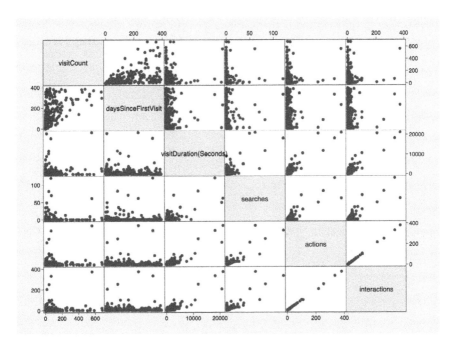

Figure 4.2 A comparison of multiple data attributes to look for patterns

These methods can also be used to assess whether different datasets are demonstrating different outcomes for particular sets of participants, or if they are likely to reflect natural variation. T-tests have several decision points. Researchers need to decide what levels of confidence they want in the results, and whether modified t-tests are appropriate where the normal distribution is not complete: maybe the values start at zero, but that is not the end of the expected curve. There are many software tools that can perform t-tests.

Regression

Regression is a technique used to identify linear patterns in data. It can find patterns to allow researchers to infer information about the population as a whole. It is a standard tool in statistical analysis and the capability to perform simple regression is readily available in many software packages including spreadsheets. However, even this relatively simple tool has multiple decision points that need to be considered to be used successfully. There are several kinds of regression techniques researchers need to choose from, and they also need to decide what data points will be used (Copus, Hübert, and Laqueur 2019, 32).

There are several ways of calculating regression, but the most common (and the default in spreadsheet packages like Microsoft Excel) is least squares regression. This is the line where the sum of the squares of the distance on the y axis between the data points and the line is smallest. This is illustrated in Figure 4.3. The issue with this method is that outliers have a disproportionate effect on the regression line because squared values increase exponentially as they get larger.

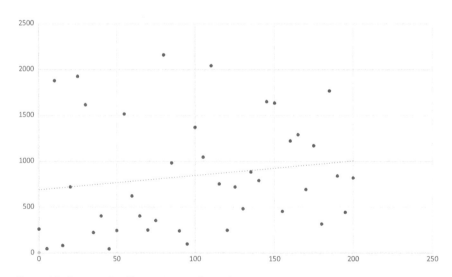

Figure 4.3 A regression line over two dimensions

There are techniques to ameliorate this issue and others that may arise, but for simple datasets it is generally sufficient.

The main use of regression is to identify patterns in numerical data, but researchers also draw in more complicated methods which can assess things like language patterns by assigning numerical values to them.

Compared to machine learning

Statistical analysis has some attributes that make it suitable for different uses than machine learning. It was developed for use with data with a few dozen variables and samples that would be considered relatively small now (Bzdok, Altman, and Krzywinski 2018). This is in contrast with machine learning, which is well suited to very large samples with many variables, furthermore:

> ML [machine learning] concentrates on prediction by using general-purpose learning algorithms to find patterns in the often rich and unwieldy data. ML methods are particularly helpful, when one is dealing with 'wide data', where the number of input variables exceeds the number of subjects, in contract to 'long data', where the number of subjects is greater than that of input variables.
>
> (Bzdok, Altman, and Krzywinski 2018)

Statistical analysis can also be done with readily available software packages, whereas machine learning requires larger datasets and more robust computer systems.

4.4 Machine learning

Machine learning is a set of techniques that can be related to the statistical methods discussed above, or it can be very different. Instead of simply identifying patterns in existing data as statistical analysis does, machine learning is designed to improve over time as more input is available. There are three main kinds of machine learning:

- Supervised learning
- Unsupervised learning
- Reinforcement learning

Machine learning is currently the most frequently discussed type of "artificial intelligence" system, and it can accept many inputs, including numerical and textual sources.

One of the main differences between statistical applications and machine learning is that in principle machine learning can be used for both prediction and inference, whereas statistical methods focus on inference based on project specific models (Bzdok, Altman, and Krzywinski 2018). In plainer terms, this means that statistical analysis allows researchers to describe a dataset as it is, but it does not give predictions of the future. In contrast, machine learning is better able to forecast future outcomes, though care still needs to be taken that the data supports them, as conditions can change after the data was collected.

This is especially the case when the data is describing human behavior, because people can respond to prior predictions. There are techniques to test how successfully predictions can be extrapolated to data that was not included in the initial training data, but generally it is important to be conservative about predicting future outcomes from existing data.

Supervised learning

In supervised learning an algorithm is presented with an existing set of labeled data and desired outputs. The goal of the process is for the application to generate rules to be followed that will continue to follow patterns identified in the data. This allows the system to continue to deliver outputs in line with those in the training data. This kind of system is often used in law to generate decision assisting technologies such as recidivism and litigation outcome predictors, but there are many possible applications.

The main limits on the adoption of supervised learning are a lack of labeled data and concerns about fairness due to biased or otherwise unfair results. Research is being done to develop ways to automate the process of labeling data, and supervised learning will be significantly more accessible once that happens. The biggest advantage to supervised learning over other methods is that supervised learning can readily provide outputs that give the criteria used to make the recommendation, which can then be evaluated. This has the potential to make machine learning more acceptable in law where process is so important. One of the main objections to the adoption of commercial systems run on these techniques is that the criteria used to make decisions are frequently treated as trade secrets and this information is not available to be examined. Required formats for supervised learning are discussed in Section 3.6.

Unsupervised learning

Unsupervised learning involves an algorithm running over data without a predetermined outcome or using tags in the data. It is used to identify patterns, and it is important for exploratory research. As an example, it could be used to identify differences in treatment between different groups in particular justice system functions without specifying what attributes would create the differences. Unsupervised learning is more accessible, because it is more accepting of different data inputs, and it can accept unlabeled data. Unfortunately, it does not usually give indications for what recommendations are based on, and without human oversight it may use inappropriate or irrelevant data for its recommendations.

Cluster analysis, which identifies the most similar results for a population to group them, is a good example of unsupervised learning. In 2019, I analyzed website interaction logs from CanLII.org to identify patterns in researcher behavior. It identified groups based on numerical values like how many times someone had visited the site in the past and how long they spent on the site to help identify patterns of user behavior that could be used to drive site development (Sutherland 2020). This project was relatively simple to complete with weblogs and commercially available software. Much more sophisticated analyses are also possible and can drive new ways of understanding patterns.

Reinforcement learning

To date, reinforcement learning has been used less in law than either supervised or unsupervised learning have. It is a technique that is used to train applications to do things like driving a car. In reinforcement learning, the system is given requirements like staying on the road and not hitting pedestrians. Then it learns how to follow the requirements in whatever way works for the system. It receives feedback as it learns and improves over time. Potential applications for reinforcement learning could include applications like writing assist technology, which could suggest the next sections or sentences in legal documents, and which would learn from whether the suggestions are accepted and how they are edited.

4.5 Natural language processing

Some of the most important developments in data use in law have come in the form of improvements to the technology and availability of natural language processing. This is because so much of the potential data that can be used in law is in the form of long written documents. See Figure 4.4 for some common uses for natural language processing.

As tools become more readily available and easier to use, natural language processing is more accessible to people who want to understand the law and legal industry better.

Simplistically, natural language processing involves collecting the data and processing it to make it consistent by removing irregularities like capital letters, irregular word endings, and stop words, which are common words and that do not add meaning (Ashley 2017, 236). This process serves to regularize the text to allow for better processing.

Once preparation of the documents is complete, there are several ways to approach processing them. Each of these is appropriate for different kinds of data and can convey different things. There are several techniques that have different levels of complexity. Many simplify language to a level that computers can parse. More in-depth discussion of two commonly used categories of techniques explored in the literature as of the time of writing follows. There are many more techniques available now and still more will be developed as the technology develops.

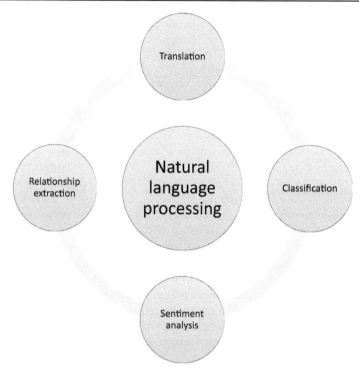

Figure 4.4 Some common uses for natural language processing

Bag-of-words

Natural language processing has made different types of research possible, especially the identification of patterns in large numbers of documents. One of the most common techniques used to date is bag-of-words. Basically in bag-of-words each word in a body of writing is taken out of context and counted. The word use can then be analyzed to draw conclusions about things like the thought patterns of the author and the ways different subjects are perceived.

Different categories of words can be selected for analysis depending on what is to be studied. Here are some examples of topics that have been explored using this technique:

- What function words are used and how (Carlson, Livermore, and Rockmore 2016)
- Word frequency (Black et al. 2016)
- Sentiment that word choice indicates about the subject (Livermore, Eidelman, and Grom 2018)

A well known example of this was reported by Sara Klingenstein, Tim Hitch-cock, and Simon DeDeo, in their article "The Civilizing Process in London's Old Bailey". It allowed them to compare word groupings that correlated with the way different kinds of criminal trials were administered. They identified a pattern of divergence between violent and non-violent offences over time among other changes (Klingenstein, Hitchcock, and DeDeo 2014, 9423).

There are limits to simple bag-of-words analysis as a tool, because in natural lan-guage word order matters. Researchers have looked at ways to combine words into larger blocks to account for word order in the analyses to resolve this (Frankenreiter and Livermore 2019, 8). This often includes treating word groups as units, so word groupings are used for analysis instead of single words. These are called *n*-grams, with *n* being the number of words that are grouped together.

Bag-of-words does have limits, as it does not account for word meanings. For example, in a court decision where one of the parties' name is "Will" about an estates matter involving a "will", bag-of-words has no way of differentiating the two meanings of the synonyms. This and other limitations have led researchers to work to develop tools that better account for meaning in analysis.

Vector analysis

One of the main vehicles researchers are exploring to move past the limitations associated with bag-of-words' limitations is vector analysis, which is often used on court judgments. It is useful because it can better preserve texts' meaning than bag-of-words does. We commonly envision vectors in two dimensions, but the vector analysis described here has many dimensions which makes it difficult for us to conceptualize what it looks like. However, this way of approaching text makes it more accessible for computers to analyze it.

In vector analysis, language is parsed to create profiles for words in multi-dimensional space by assigning numerical values based on how they relate to other words. These numerical values are then treated as vectors, or dimensional forces, that move in particular directions. They are then graphed using compu-ter programs. This can demonstrate relationships between terms: vector analy-sis can show parallel concepts and identify analogy: the closer terms are to each other the more related they are (Garg et al. 2018).

The advantage of vector analysis is that "vector representations of words and documents are information dense — in the sense of retaining information about the semantic content and meaning — while also being computationally tract-able" (Ash and Chen 2019, 313). As an example, vector analysis found that the vector values for "corporate income tax" – "corporation" + "person" = "per-sonal income tax" (Ash 2015, 19).

Presenting data in the form of vectors can also make bias apparent where it is embedded in language: "Paris" is in the same place in relation to "France" as "London" is to "England", but "Doctor" is also in the same place in rela-tion to "man" as "nurse" is to "woman". This encoded bias is basically the "computational analogue to the Implicit Association Test" (Soh 2020), as it shows the underlying bias that authors bring to their writing. It will be necessary to find ways to resolve these issues if vector analysis is going to be widely adopted in law, as it is not appropriate to develop automated legal systems that encode these biases without ways to remediate for them.

4.6 Other tools

The previous tools are the ones that are most commonly discussed in the research literature relating to legal data, but they are certainly not the only possibilities. There are many tools that get less attention, which are well used and should not be forgotten, especially when organizations are looking to present their data for use in processes. Just because certain technologies are not fashionable does not mean they are not useful.

Many of the other tools used with legal data focus less on analysis and more on presenting data in usable ways. The following is not intended to be an exhaustive list of techniques to manipulate and manage legal data. Rather these examples have been selected to give some idea of potential tools and as a starting point to find the right one for given situations. There are many more tools that are available for understanding data.

These three tools demonstrate ways to approach three important research and business needs, but there are more that can be explored based on a particular situation:

Knowledge bases

Knowledge bases were some of the main tools that were anticipated to drive artificial intelligence development in the 1980s. They present existing information in a structured way, and they can be useful ways to present data associated with known information. Common examples of knowledge bases are knowledge management and expert systems. One of the main concerns about knowledge bases is that it is difficult to maintain their currency. As with other applications, it is also problematic to encode the concrete rules computer systems require when legal concepts like "reasonableness" may not be explicitly defined (Ashley 2017, 10).

Knowledge bases continue to be important as ways for organizations to store and share their data and information, though in many contexts the internet has overtaken the role of internal knowledge bases. This mature technology has value to offer given the right use cases and adequate commitment of resources and effort to populate and maintain it properly.

Decision trees

Decision trees are another mature technique that is useful for assessing value and presenting information. They are populated with known points where

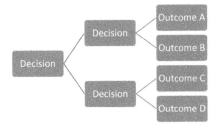

Figure 4.5 A simple decision tree

decisions or events can affect outcomes with estimated values or likely outcomes related to each option. They can be used to convey information in complex situations and as discussion tools to invite input from others and make assumptions explicit. They can be portrayed using graphs like the one displayed in Figure 4.6. That decision tree is simple, but they can be as complex as required. It is common to include estimated probabilities of various outcomes and monetary outcomes to help assess the value of different courses of action. In many cases complex decision trees are integrated into systems that allow users to navigate based on their circumstances without displaying the full structure at once.

There are commercially available and custom programs that support decision trees for presenting information to users based on their particular needs. These have been widely adopted in the legal non-profit sector as efficient tools to support unrepresented litigants who need customized information. They have also been recommended as tools in mediation and litigation:

> Some skilled mediators routinely use decision trees. They draw a flow chart on a board with input from counsel and the parties during the mediation. Typically, the decision tree will reveal hidden, yet powerful, information about the case, such as the statistical chances of being successful on a given issue (many of which end up invariably lower than what counsel and clients anticipated), and the cost of failing on any given issue (many of which are invariably higher than anticipated). (Canadian Lawyer 2014)

Tools like decision trees can give insights into projected outcomes, which can be based on monetary values, or they can be based on other attributes such as time. The availability of better data will provide improved estimates for use in tools like decision trees into the future. These tools are well used in business, and they can also be deployed in many applications in law where decision points are important. My analysis of a hypothetical law practice and the value of improved information based on decision tree analysis shows that small differences in the quality of information used in advice given to clients would have significant impacts on the expected value of those matters (Sutherland 2017).

Network analysis

Network analysis is another mature tool for research and assessment. Network analysis is the study of the patterns created by relationships between things. They have many uses, for instance, they are used by management consultants to assess organizational cultures. This assessment can help them understand the dynamics in their organizations better and identify key people within organizations, as many of these people are not necessarily in key positions in the organizational chart.

Analysis of citation relationships between documents, especially court decisions is another important application. Legal publishers do this to assist in applications such as developing automated classification, and academic researchers use it to demonstrate patterns in the law. For example, Badawi and Dari-Mattiacci used references to sections within several countries' civil codes to better understand the influence countries had on each other as they developed their laws. Known historical exchanges were mirrored in the structure of the references (Badawi and Dari-Mattiacci 2019).

4.7 Conclusion

It is safe to say that there will continue to be new tools to analyze data emerging over time, which will be useful in legal scholarship and practice. Many of them will be based on the paradigms listed above, but some will be different. These developments are dealt with at more length in Chapter 9 but most of these new tools are unlikely to be so far outside the existing state of the art that they could not be anticipated. It takes time for new tools to be developed, applied to a discipline, commercialized, and adopted by users. This gives us time to prepare if we pay attention.

Much of the low hanging fruit in data analysis is now being harvested, as participants in the legal space explore the potential to apply existing tools that have been developed in other areas. The plethora of opportunities, paired with the increased cultural openness to technology tools, is making change go quickly. Whether the next set of developments will be as easy to identify and implement remains to be seen: some applications are easier to use than others, with some becoming very accessible, while others still several years away from development. One thing that is likely to happen is that less expertise in computing will be required to analyze and understand data in the future. More software tools designed for use with data and data driven information products are being made available all the time, and this is a good time to explore.

Finding the best way to interpret a particular text with particular goals in mind takes creativity (Frankenreiter and Livermore 2019, 9). The tools mentioned here and others that are currently in use or may be adopted and developed in time will help to validate many research hypotheses that could not be corroborated without them, and make many processes and systems feasible that were previously not considered. That said they are not panaceas. They may be helpful in identifying patterns in existing data, but the work of validating hypotheses about what will happen in the future cannot be delegated to computer systems. It is necessary to estimate levels of confidence based on the data and information we have access to using our own knowledge and intuition (Webb 2016, 230).

Works cited

Ash, Elliott. 2015. "The Political Economy of Tax Laws in the U.S. States." https://api.semanticscholar.org/CorpusID:9658318.

Ash, Elliott, and Daniel L. Chen. 2019. "Case Vectors: Spatial Representations of the Law Using Document Embeddings." In *Law as Data: Computation, Text, and the Future of Legal Analysis*, 313–337. The SFI Press Seminar Series. Santa Fe: The SFI Press.

Ashley, Kevin D. 2017. *Artificial Intelligence and Legal Analytics: New Tools for Law Practice in the Digital Age*. Cambridge: Cambridge University Press.

Badawi, Adam B., and Giuseppe Dari-Mattiacci. 2019. "Reference Networks and Civil Codes." In *Law as Data: Computation, Text, and the Future of Legal Analysis*, 339–365. The SFI Press Seminar Series. Santa Fe: The SFI Press.

Black, Ryan C., Ryan J. Owens, Justin Wedeking, and Patrick C. Wohlfarth. 2016. "The Influence of Public Sentiment on Supreme Court Opinion Clarity." *Law & Society Review* 50 (3): 703–732. https://doi.org/10.1111/lasr.12219.

Bzdok, Danilo, Naomi Altman, and Martin Krzywinski. 2018. "Statistics Versus Machine Learning." *Nature Methods* 15 (4): 233–234. https://doi.org/10.1038/nmeth.4642.

Canadian Lawyer. 2014. "Here's to Using Decision Trees in the New Year." 2014. https://www.canadianlawyermag.com/practice-areas/adr/heres-to-using-decision-trees-in-the-new-year/269264.

Carlson, Keith, Michael Livermore, and Daniel Rockmore. 2016. "A Quantitative Analysis of Writing Style on the U.S. Supreme Court." *Washington University Law Review* 93 (6): 1461–1510.

Copus, Ryan, Ryan Hübert, and Hannah Laqueur. 2019. "Big Data, Machine Learning, and the Credibility Revolution in Empirical Legal Studies." In *Law as Data: Computation, Text, and the Future of Legal Analysis*, 21–57. The SFI Press Seminar Series. Santa Fe: The SFI Press.

Dumas, Marion, and Jens Frankenreiter. 2019. "Text as Observational Data." In *Law as Data: Computation, Text, and the Future of Legal Analysis*, 59–70. The SFI Press Seminar Series. Santa Fe: The SFI Press.

Frankenreiter, Jens, and Michael A. Livermore. 2019. "Computational Methods in Legal Analysis." SSRN Scholarly Paper ID 3568558. Rochester, NY: Social Science Research Network. https://papers.ssrn.com/abstract=3568558.

Garg, Nikhil, Londa Schiebinger, Dan Jurafsky, and James Zou. 2018. "Word Embeddings Quantify 100 Years of Gender and Ethnic Stereotypes." *Proceedings of the National Academy of Sciences* 115 (16): E3635–3644. https://doi.org/10.1073/pnas.1720347115.

Holmes, Jr., Oliver Wendell. 1897. "The Path of the Law." *Harvard Law Review* 10: 457.

Klingenstein, Sara, Tim Hitchcock, and Simon DeDeo. 2014. "The Civilizing Process in London's Old Bailey." *Proceedings of the National Academy of Sciences* 111 (26): 9419–9424. https://doi.org/10.1073/pnas.1405984111.

Livermore, Michael A, Vladimir Eidelman, and Brian Grom. 2018. "Computationally Assisted Regulatory Participation." *Notre Dame Law Review* 93: 977–1034.

Livermore, Michael A., and Daniel N. Rockmore. 2019. "Distant Reading the Law." In *Law as Data: Computation, Text, and the Future of Legal Analysis*, 3–19. The SFI Press Seminar Series. Santa Fe: The SFI Press.

Soh, Jerrold. 2020. "When Are Algorithms Biased? A Multi-Disciplinary Survey." SSRN Scholarly Paper ID 3602662. Rochester, NY: Social Science Research Network. https://doi.org/10.2139/ssrn.3602662.

Sutherland, Sarah. 2017. "Quantifying the Value of Legal Information." *Slaw* (blog). June 1, 2017. http://www.slaw.ca/2017/06/01/quantifying-the-value-of-legal-information/.

Sutherland, Sarah. 2020. "Exploration of Attributes Associated with User Behaviour in Online Legal Research." *Canadian Law Library Review* 45 (2): 10–13.

Underwood, Ted. 2019. *Distant Horizons: Digital Evidence and Literary Change*. Chicago: University of Chicago Press. https://www.amazon.ca/Distant-Horizons-Digital-Evidence-Literary/dp/022661283X/ref=tmm_pap_swatch_0?_encoding=UTF8&qid=&sr=.

Washington University Law. n.d. *"The Supreme Court Database."* Accessed August 2, 2020. http://scdb.wustl.edu/.

Webb, Amy. 2016. *The Signals Are Talking: Why Today's Fringe Is Tomorrow's Mainstream*. New York: PublicAffairs.

Chapter 5

Interpreting legal data

5.1 Introduction

There are many ways to interpret data. It is possible to get some answers from data by simply looking at it or by plotting it on a graph, such as whether visits to a website or a number of court decisions in a particular area are trending up or down since last year. In other instances, it may not be clear if the differences show a pattern or if they can just be explained by random variability. In others still, the data may be so complex that without advanced tools it can be difficult to even identify aspects of data that can be analyzed, never mind understanding what they might mean.

Deciding how to approach legal issues using data requires understanding both the law and analysis techniques. In many cases, it is more difficult to get a dataset that reflects the target than it is to analyze it once it has been obtained. Consider the example of case law: beyond the issues that may be faced in getting access to it in a usable format, what does a body of published case law document? Traditionally it has been used to provide a narrative about what gave rise to the action, what happened in court, and an explanation of why a decision was made. Accessing the courts and writing judgments is expensive and time consuming, so routine disputes are channeled toward alternatives to litigation like private settlements and mediation, or they are dealt with orally, so the decision documents may never be published. This means they primarily provide guidance on outlying issues, while simpler and cheaper methods are preferred for deciding matters where the law is clear.

Even when matters go to court, there are often not written decisions available for any number of reasons. For example, analysis of publication patterns for different case law databases in the United Kingdom found that different platforms have significant variation in the volume of decisions published, which would significantly affect the results of any kind of research using them (Hoadley 2018). The decisions were missing primarily because many oral decisions that had a different process for publication were missing in some places. Being sophisticated in approaching these challenges is necessary for projects to be successful. There are ways to approach these goals based on what data is

DOI: 10.4324/9781003127307-5

available. Some of the most common considerations for how to select a methodology follow.

5.2 Approaching data analysis

As discussed in Chapter 2, even experts find it surprisingly difficult to do something as apparently simple as counting how many times something happened when collecting statistical data (Spiegelhalter 2019, 20), so it is important to consider carefully what approach to take early in the process — ideally before data is collected. Data analysis requires critical thinking about how to approach problems, such as what kinds of problems can be solved with better information and what kinds of data could give an answer to a key question. Data derived information can be valuable for many reasons: it may illuminate an issue that is not clear, it may be valuable to understand a situation better, or it may facilitate making better decisions.

A limiting aspect of analyzing legal data is that in many instances data collection is a secondary consideration in its creation. Lawyers do things like generate documents and record information about hours to be billed as part of their work, but the processes involved are designed to do things like furthering the interests of clients and ensuring a law firm runs a successful business. Courts accumulate dockets and judgements as they adjudicate matters, but these processes are designed to ensure they communicate rulings clearly, adjudicate appropriately, and maintain records of good process. These processes and their underlying priorities mean that there will always be missing data from the perspective of a data analyst. Frequently the quality and quantity of data associated with adjudicative processes are so poor that research projects looking into them need to be abandoned (Salter 2021).

Situations where adequate data is not created during regular processes may open opportunities for experimentation. Developing controlled experiments can better illuminate issues and identify the sources of different outcomes, but part of the problem with the investigation of data relating to the legal system is a lack of a culture of experimentation in law.

Experimental methods set up situations where everything is kept as similar as possible and only one element is changed. This creates datasets that can be compared: those that had the intervention and those that did not. These can then be used to assess what changes occurred and isolate the causes. However, there has been resistance to doing things like taking a random sample of people in particular jurisdictions and assigning them to be governed by different laws and comparing the results. The primary argument against this is that the best governance model should apply to everyone, but currently laws are changed for everyone in a jurisdiction with no validation that the change is beneficial (Lynch, Greiner, and Cohen 2020).

A major reason that data is not available is because there is no counter-factual data available — it is impossible to know what might have but did not happen (Hand 2020). Experimental methodologies are designed to develop counter-factual data to compare outcomes, but extensive experimentation is particularly challenging in law. In this way, it is similar to geology: physicists and chemists can look at a moment in time and ascertain what they perceive to be universal laws, but geologists cannot look at the earth without the complication of millions of years passing (Bjornerud 2018).

The same comparison can be made between psychologists and sociologists looking at a particular moment in time, and legal scholars and historians who cannot separate the present from the past. There are no counterfactuals, only what happened. It is impossible to separate a legal system or a legal organization from the long timelines over which societies exist. Even relatively new countries tend to adopt the legal traditions of those that came before or look to others for templates:

• Countries with civil codes, such as Austria, Italy, Germany, and Spain, use other countries' codes as templates (Badawi and Dari-Mattiacci 2019)
• When colonies become independent they frequently carry over the laws that were in place before and amend them from there

5.3 Methodology

There are three main categories of methods used to approach legal data that will be covered in this book: statistical analysis, machine learning, and natural language processing. These were selected with the goal of giving an overarching view of the field, and the list is not intended to be exhaustive. The categories are also not exclusive of each other: machine learning may be used in natural language processing and both may be used in conjunction with statistical methods.

There are many more possible ways to approach these issues, in fact they are limited only by the creativity of the people doing the research with more possibilities opening regularly as developments in other fields become well enough developed that they can be deployed by legal researchers.

Statistics

At their most simple, statistical methods use numerical information to analyze data. Unlike in some other fields, in law there is often limited numerical information available without parsing natural language or custom collection. This both drives, and is the result of, a limited culture of data use in law outside certain subject areas that easily lend themselves to it, such as sentence lengths and damages amounts. Statistical analysis signals a change from an ideal where each individual situation is judged on its merits using reason. There are many statistical techniques that can be used, but the two that are most common, and which include many other techniques under their umbrellas, are hypothesis testing and regression.

Hypothesis testing

Statistical hypothesis testing allows researchers to use a statistical test to ascertain if a dataset conforms to what would be expected if the hypothesis were true. A hypothesis for these tests can be as simple as "I don't think this intervention will have any effect on outcomes" or "I think this variation in inputs will lead to a different outcome." The tests generally require understanding the structure of the data and effective sampling to give accurate results.

The most commonly used tests for hypotheses are called t-tests, which were introduced in Section 4.3. Basically they compare averages between two samples to tell how statistically likely it is for the differences between them to be random. There are many considerations, including what type of test to choose, how to sample the data, and what confidence level is acceptable. Once these decisions are made and the test is run, it will give a p-value, which tells how probable it is for the data in question to be generated if the hypothesis is true. It is important to understand that t-tests are not testing if the hypothesis is true. They are testing if the data is consistent with the hypothesis being true:

> The p-value is a horribly misunderstood concept. People often think it gives the probability that the hypothesis is either right or wrong. It does not. The hypothesis is either right or wrong, and the p-value simply tells you the probability of getting certain extreme outcomes if right.
>
> (Hand 2020, 193)

Regression

Another set of techniques that can help with data analysis is regression, regression was also discussed in Chapter 4. It delivers a trend line that may be used for applications like the identification of patterns for values over a range such as date, income levels, or duration. Regression over two dimensions is easy to graph and gives the familiar image of a scatter plot of data points and a trend line. More complicated analyses are also computationally possible, because computers are not limited to visualizing two or three dimensions as people are. There are many programs available that can calculate regression over multiple dimensions.

Spreadsheet software include the capacity to do simple regression, but like many software programs they will run the math whether the data being processed is suitable for the data or not. To avoid issues, it can be useful to look at a graph of the data to see if it looks like it follows a linear pattern. There are many possibilities beyond straight lines, such as curved, parabolic, or wavy lines. Data may also follow one pattern over one portion of the range then change at a certain value, changing angle or jumping to a different value range at that point. The data points may also have a random or non-linear distribution, in which case using regression is inappropriate.

Machine learning

Machine learning is the use of specialized computer algorithms that can process large amounts of data and identify patterns in them. One of the most important elements of machine learning applications is that they can "learn", which is to say that are able to improve their analysis as more data becomes available.

Statistics started to emerge as a discipline in the 18th century, but machine learning is much newer. It grew out of improved statistical techniques and initial research into machine learning in the 1950s, and after approximately 60 years of development it became flexible enough to use for many different applications. Since then it has reached the point of being widely used in commercial applications and academic fields like law.

Some companies now make their platforms available for third parties to use, and it has become accessible for moderately well funded projects and organization to use machine learning to deal with legal documents. Machine learning algorithms tend to handle datasets with long data, or data with large numbers of data points in each document or item being compared, better than traditional techniques like regression (Frankenreiter and Livermore 2019, 15). This is especially important for analyses of legal documents which can be hundreds of pages long. This is discussed further below in Section 5.4.

There are two kinds of machine learning algorithms. The first uses algorithms to generate variables that can be used for statistical applications like regression analysis. The second applies algorithms to textual data to allow researchers to identify patterns. They can give answers to questions like: "given a set of variables x, what is the likely outcome of y?" However, machine learning algorithms were not designed to find the causes of particular outcomes, and they are generally not well suited for that purpose (Dumas and Frankenreiter 2019, 62–3).

Natural language

One of the most important areas of improvement for data analysis in the legal space is in better natural language processing. Superior techniques for parsing free text and extracting data elements has made it considerably easier to convert text into formats that computers can use, whether by extracting numerical data or converting the text itself into formats that can be analyzed such as n-grams or vectors, see Chapter 4 for a more in-depth discussion of these topics. This means that analyses that are too daunting or impossibly voluminous to manage manually can now be assessed using automated programs.

The reason it is valuable to covert natural language into numerical or other computationally tractable values is because this makes them easier to compute. That said, while having sophisticated techniques that convert legal texts to data has many advantages, they also raise their own challenges. It is important to carefully consider the tradeoffs associated with the choices that are required to run these systems when considering a particular question (Frankenreiter and Livermore 2019, 5).

Many of these methods were developed by researchers working in computer science, and then they were used by scholars in the digital humanities before they were adopted into legal applications. The fact that these tools have been in use for some time means that they are now well developed and much less effort is required to apply them than would be required if they were being developed for this use only.

5.4 Considerations

Understanding these issues better and demanding better data practices will help ensure that best practices are followed. It is important for people to understand what is driving the applications and research results they use and what their limitations are.

Correlation and causation

One of the major concerns about analysis is how to identify the difference between correlation and causation. Correlation means that different attributes in a dataset change together but may not be caused by each other, like high summer temperatures and sales of beach balls. Causation means that things not only change together, but that they also are caused by each other in some way, like summer rain and plant growth.

Identification of causation is difficult, and generally it requires counter-factual data and controlled conditions to isolate. This is where a culture of experimentation in law would be helpful, as different scenarios could be carried out and causes could be isolated. It is easy to mistake correlation for causation and use correlated data points rather than causative data points without realizing it is happening. In fact, without experimental methodologies that isolate causes, it is only possible to measure correlation. It is frequently easier to measure correlated data points, so it is easier to use them in models. If only data from life is available, it is impossible to know for certain what causes certain outcomes (Dumas and Frankenreiter 2019, 60).

As an example, in law firms it is common to evaluate performance of lawyers by how many hours they bill, but billable hours are only correlated with profitability they are not causative: many hours worked are written off and not billed to clients, or perhaps clients do not see value in the work done and refuse to pay. If lawyers do not know where the real value of what they do is for clients and the business, they may think that billing more hours demonstrates their contributions to profitability where in fact it is secondary. It is just the easiest thing to measure.

To use another example with real world implications, one important use for legal data is demonstrating systems of justice and fairness or injustice and unfairness. By quantifying outcomes for different groups, this can identify patterns where justice is done and when it is not. That said, it is not always clear what causes a particular correlated outcome.

For example, calculating differences between the number of people of different groups in prison is insufficiently nuanced to understand crime rates or alternatively to find the causes of inequalities in outcomes. Underlying patterns could be caused by things like:

- Increased policing in particular neighborhoods or communities
- Less willingness to give some individuals the benefit of second and third chances
- Increased likelihood of being indicted in the same circumstances
- Different levels of pressure to take deal offers
- Bias on the part of decision makers at each stage of the process

These are all possible causes that would be missed if only the correlated patterns in prison populations were analyzed, and they do not require any differences in patterns of behavior in the underlying population. Increased likelihood of being in jail is correlated with both crime rates and injustice, and it can make a strong case that injustice is happening, but it is difficult to narrow down the ultimate cause.

These patterns can be concentrated in artificial intelligence driven systems that use corelative data from prior patterns in the justice system to generate outcomes that affect real people now. Predictive tools are being taught using arrest data to model criminal activity, because that is what police departments have data for but arrests do not always lead to convictions or follow crimes (Heaven 2020).

Proxy data

Creating a plan to find a proxy for the thing to be measured is a sophisticated way to approach the issue of correlation and causation. Using a proxy is the conscious choice to use correlated data points when causative data points are unavailable or difficult to measure. This is especially relevant in textual analysis: "Information in legal documents can also serve as proxies for other facts that cannot be directly observed." (Frankenreiter and Livermore 2019, 15)

It is crucial to be conscious that a decision is being made to use a proxy, and what can legitimately be derived from the results and what cannot. It is especially important to consider if incentives are attached to a proxy that may reward distortionary behavior. This can diminish the value of the proxy to measure the underlying values. If judges are confronted with statistics on their performance and evaluated on analytics for example, it may encourage them to try to manipulate their data (McGill and Salyzyn 2021, 18).

Sensitivity

Sensitivity is how responsive outputs are to changes in input. When data changes there can be different results. In some cases, there is little difference in outputs. In others there are large differences in output generated by relatively similar inputs. Modern data analysis methods tend to be sensitive, and new data points or changes require analyses to be rerun, because they can change the whole output.

In 2017, Daniel Martin Katz, Michael J. Bommarito II, and Josh Blackman published a paper about their application for predicting outcomes for decisions in the Supreme Court of the United States. Their model found that when making predictions of that nature any change in the initial conditions changed the prediction. For example, if a delay occurred in a predicted hearing date, the delay measure was increased, and they reran the analysis to get a different prediction (Katz, Bommarito, II, and Blackman 2017).

This was not using data that was not available before the decision is issued. It is just updating the existing initial conditions as they change over time. This is important because some of the desired attributes for prediction applications is that they work for new data that is available into the future which does not have an outcome yet. Identification of patterns within data that is complete with all outcomes already known may not allow for prediction if it is only applicable to that particular dataset.

Suitability

Available data may not meet the requirements for particular needs, such as informing decision making. For example, law firms may not be collecting the data needed to make better business decisions or know what areas of practice are most profitable. In these cases, some thought can be put into what kinds of questions can be answered with available or possible data and how it can most effectively be collected. Some new practice management tools allow for extraction of analytics about the business and some guidance on how they can be used.

In social science research, it is also important to consider suitability for use and issues with sampling. Understanding what available data is evidence of can avoid many problems. If the main data source being used is a case law corpus for example, it may not be possible to draw conclusions about all the people who are faced with a particular legal issue, because they might not all have gone to trial or had written decisions published about their cases.

In these situations, it may be necessary to analyze what is available, and what additional data could be collected that would fill in gaps. When deciding what data to collect it is important to evaluate how useful it will be, and what it can or cannot say.

Complexity

One of the reasons there has been relatively slow adoption of analytical techniques in law is because of the complexity involved in analyzing them. The length of the documents and the sophistication of the language involved has meant that the techniques needed to be well developed before they could be applied:

Legal documents are natively very high dimensional objects. For example, if texts are treated as an ordered sequence of words, the dimensionality of such a representation would be extremely high: documents that were 1000 words long in a simple language with a vocabulary of 1000 words would be represented in a space of 10^{3000} dimensions.

(Frankenreiter and Livermore 2019, 6)

In addition to the complexity within the documents themselves, there is also network complexity as legal documents have extensive citation networks. These networks serve to mark particular documents as important, but they also point to particular sections and topics within them. Highly cited cases may include information about many topics, but they are not typically considered to be important for all of them. It is necessary to deal with this complexity to successfully understand and fully leverage their full potential as data.

Extrapolation

It seems clear that correlated data will continue to be used in research and commercial applications for the foreseeable future, and there is demand for systems that will provide prediction for events that have not happened yet. These uses require extrapolation to design systems that will support them. This may be an acceptable use of the data if it is used in sophisticated ways and does not make claims that are not supported, though it is sensitive and will need to be watched closely.

One necessity for a successful prediction generator is that it needs to work using data that is outside the initial set used to train it. If it only works for the initial sample, then it is not useful except as a proof of concept. This is called out of sample fit, and projects should be designed to ensure that they continue to work as new data becomes available. In a case predictor, all knowledge required to make a prediction should be available before the decision is issued (Katz, Bommarito, and Blackman 2017).

As extrapolation using legal data becomes more sophisticated and widely adopted, it will be necessary to remember that quantified legal prediction only simulates legal decision making: instead it processes data not content or meaning. If machine learning is adopted further into the legal space, lawyers will need to develop new skills to assess machine learning recommendations fairly (Hildebrandt 2017, 12–13).

5.5 Concerns

Choosing the right tool for a task is important. Especially because many computer programs will give outputs as long as certain minimum requirements for data format are met regardless of the suitability of the tool for the dataset. Without thinking critically about what is being asked and what the data supports, this can lead to confidence where it should not exist. Spreadsheet software will assign a regression line to a random set of data points, which is relatively easy to see. Other inappropriate uses may not be as apparent, especially if they involve more complex data and applications.

Machine learning in particular can be opaque. Many organizations seek to use trade secrets to protect their innovations, which limit outsiders' ability to verify the validity of their systems. There is some speculation that in time applications used in public legal contexts may be required use open source software to mitigate this issue.

There is also opacity between law and computer science as disciplines with practitioners of each not fully understanding the other. Computer scientists frequently do not understand the rule of law and legal scholars do not understand the vocabulary of computer science (Hildebrandt 2017, 12). Over time this may change, but in the meantime it limits the oversight of tools that have important implications for people's lives, especially in areas of law with higher rates of unrepresented and poor participants like the criminal justice system and immigration law.

Given the emerging concerns about data analysis driven applications and decision making in law and the damage they can do, there will almost certainly be increased regulation in at least some parts of the world. However, it appears that the importance of training data in machine learning techniques and how easily it can create biased outcomes suggests that training data should be regulated in preference over algorithms. In the European Union three particular areas of risk related to data systems have been identified which could be addressed by regulation. They include:

- Risks arising from data quality
- Risks associated with discrimination embedded in these systems
- Risks associated with limits on innovation arising from intellectual property rights or over restrictive regulation (Hacker 2020, 2).

In addition to the above general concerns, there are also the following issues.

Overfitting

It is possible to generate models that closely reflect sample data, which then perform badly on other samples from the same set, this is known as overfitting (Copus, Hübert, and Laqueur 2019, 33). Overfitting is a data analysis error that involves making a model fit a particular sample too closely. It happens when a model has extra terms which make it fit random variation in the data rather than real patterns. This means that if any data point is taken out of the sample it could be put back in the same place using the model, but it does not say anything about data outside the sample. Essentially the model memorizes the training data instead of learning a generalization from it. A model like this will

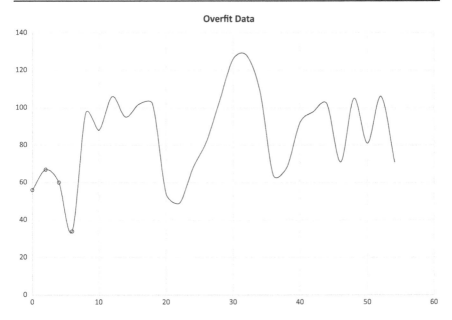

Figure 5.1 An example of overfit data

fail when making predictions about new data (Ashley 2017, 113). Figure 5.1 shows an example of an overfit trendline.

Bias

Bias is a significant issue for applications based on legal data. It is impossible to look at any set of data that has been built over long timelines and not have historical information that may not reflect how society wants decisions to be made now, and this is being charitable that contemporary data will not also include unwanted bias. Anyone using text analysis tools to study law must consider the problems associated with biased data in the corpus of published legal documents (Carlson, Livermore, and Rockmore 2020, 228). Section 7.8 includes further discussion of bias and how it can affect data driven systems.

5.6 Conclusion

It is important to assess whether available data is sufficient when deciding how to analyze data, and if it is possible to get more to fill any gaps. It can also be just as crucial to know when to stop collecting data as it is to know how to find and interpret it. It is necessary to make decisions based on imperfect data as there is always data missing. All data by definition is imperfect. It can never tell everything about a situation. Just as there are limits to human reason, there are limits to analysis based on data, and it is important to understand them. These questions and challenges are not new. In 1897 Oliver Wendell Holmes wrote:

> The means of the study are a body of reports, of treatises, and of statutes, in this country and in England, extending back for six hundred years, and now increasing annually by hundreds. In these sibylline leaves are gathered the scattered prophecies of the past upon the cases in which the axe will fall. These are what properly have been called the oracles of the law. Far the most important and pretty nearly the whole meaning of every new effort of legal thought is to make these prophecies more precise, and to generalize them into a thoroughly connected system.
>
> (Holmes 1897)

It can be hoped that the new tools being adopted will facilitate moving toward a better system for understanding the law and how people interact with it. That said, accurately answering critical questions about factual assertions is and is likely to continue to be a difficult problem. It is necessary to know what questions to ask in each context, and in law this is the job of human experts. Computational systems will likely never be able to do this, but they are and will almost certainly continue to be useful models to test assumptions (Ashley 2017, 147).

Works cited

Ashley, Kevin D. 2017. *Artificial Intelligence and Legal Analytics: New Tools for Law Practice in the Digital Age*. Cambridge: Cambridge University Press.

Badawi, Adam B., and Giuseppe Dari-Mattiacci. 2019. "Reference Networks and Civil Codes." In *Law as Data: Computation, Text, and the Future of Legal Analysis*, 339–365. The SFI Press Seminar Series. Santa Fe: The SFI Press.

Bjornerud, Marcia. 2018. *Timefulness: How Thinking Like a Geologist Can Help Save the World*. Princeton, NJ: Princeton University Press.

Carlson, Keith, Michael A. Livermore, and Daniel N. Rockmore. 2020. "The Problem of Data Bias in the Pool of Published U.S. Appellate Court Opinions." *Journal of Empirical Legal Studies* 17 (2): 224–261. https://doi.org/10.1111/jels.12253.

Copus, Ryan, Ryan Hübert, and Hannah Laqueur. 2019. "Big Data, Machine Learning, and the Credibility Revolution in Empirical Legal Studies." In *Law as Data: Computation, Text, and the Future of Legal Analysis*, 21–57. The SFI Press Seminar Series. Santa Fe: The SFI Press.

Dumas, Marion, and Jens Frankenreiter. 2019. "Text as Observational Data." In *Law as Data: Computation, Text, and the Future of Legal Analysis*, 59–70. The SFI Press Seminar Series. Santa Fe: The SFI Press.

Frankenreiter, Jens, and Michael A. Livermore. 2019. "*Computational Methods in Legal Analysis*." SSRN Scholarly Paper ID 3568558. Rochester, NY: Social Science Research Network. https://papers.ssrn.com/abstract=3568558.

Hacker, Philipp. 2020. "A Legal Framework for AI Training Data." SSRN Scholarly Paper ID 3556598. Rochester, NY: Social Science Research Network. https://doi.org/10.2139/ssrn.3556598.

Hand, David J. 2020. *Dark Data: Why What You Don't Know Matters*. Princeton: Princeton University Press.

Heaven, Will Douglas. 2020. "Predictive Policing Algorithms Are Racist. They Need to Be Dismantled." *MIT Technology Review*. July 17, 2020. https://www.technologyreview.com/2020/07/17/1005396/predictive-policing-algorithms-racist-dismantled-machine-learning-bias-criminal-justice/.

Hildebrandt, Mireille. 2017. "Law As Computation in the Era of Artificial Legal Intelligence. Speaking Law to the Power of Statistics." SSRN Scholarly Paper ID 2983045. Rochester, NY: Social Science Research Network. https://doi.org/10.2139/ssrn.2983045.

Hoadley, Daniel. 2018. "Part 2: Open Access to English Case Law (The Gaps)." *CARREFAX* (blog). May 10, 2018. http://carrefax.com/articles-blog/2018/5/9/part-2-open-access-to-english-case-law-knackered-plumbing.

Holmes, Jr., and Oliver Wendell. 1897. "The Path of the Law." *Harvard Law Review* 10: 457.

Katz, Daniel Martin, Michael J. Bommarito, II, and Josh Blackman. 2017. "A General Approach for Predicting the Behavior of the Supreme Court of the United States." *PLOS ONE* 12 (4): e0174698. https://doi.org/10.1371/journal.pone.0174698.

Lynch, H. Fernandez, D. J. Greiner, and I. G. Cohen. 2020. "Overcoming Obstacles to Experiments in Legal Practice." *Science* 367 (6482): 1078–1080. https://doi.org/10.1126/science.aay3005.

McGill, Jena, and Amy Salyzyn. 2021. "Judging by Numbers: How Will Judicial Analytics Impact the Justice System and Its Stakeholders?" *Dalhousie Law Journal* 44 (1): (Forthcoming).

Salter, Shannon. 2021. (Chair at Civil Resolution Tribunal of British Columbia, and adjunct professor at the UBC Allard School of Law), in discussion with the author.

Spiegelhalter, David. 2019. *The Art of Statistics: Learning from Data*. New York: Viking.

Chapter 6

Issues with using legal data

6.1 Introduction

The increased use of data in the legal system has been much anticipated with both positive and negative effects expected. Among other anticipated outcomes, people look forward to the development and adoption of systems that promise much delayed productivity gains, which they hope will reduce the cost of legal services, thereby bringing improved access to justice for more people. At the same time, many are apprehensive that these changes will create new sources of injustice they cannot anticipate, and that there will be losses of employment and income for many current participants in the legal system. Both these hopes and concerns are warranted.

Most of the applications and systems anticipated to transform the legal system are driven by data in one form or another, and creating custom datasets to be used as inputs is frequently prohibitively expensive. This means that many actors in this space are looking to access datasets that already exist. However, there are frequently issues with data not being available in desired formats and with suitable licensing. There are also concerns about the suitability of available data for use in many of the applications that people want to create. These concerns will need to be addressed and understood if the projected changes are to happen in the ways people want.

6.2 Availability

Before considering what data does not exist or is not recorded yet, it is useful to consider the data that exists now and how or if it is available for particular analyses. The availability of primary law in the form of court documents and legislation is a major issue in the pursuit of a legal system that is more responsive to quantitative methods, though to what extent it is an issue varies around the world. While almost all courts and legislative bodies make their documents available to be published for use by individuals doing legal research, many see their current modes of distribution as adequate and may not wish to increase them to allow for further analysis. Recent examples include the State of Georgia's litigation to stop Carl

DOI: 10.4324/9781003127307-6

Malamud and Public.Resource.Org from publishing the *Official Code of Georgia Annotated* in the United States (Georgia et al. v. Public.Resource.Org, Inc. 2020) and a law introduced in 2019 in France which prohibits the publication of statistical analysis of court decisions (Légifrance 2019).

Beyond the availability of legal documents, there are also often limits on the availability of information on analysis that is done, especially that which is carried out by companies. Researchers in these organizations may not publish their research, and even where they do publish about their enquiries, it is common for them not to include enough detail in their articles to allow others to reproduce their work. To reproduce machine learning techniques in particular requires the code involved in the project, but also details about the dataset, metadata, and detailed instructions. It is the norm in academic communication that scientific articles include enough detail to recreate the work, but this frequently runs into conflict with the commercial interests of the companies funding the research. This is understandable, but it is not conducive to scientific communication (Heaven 2020).

6.3 What is missing

Even where governments have the best intentions of making data available, it is inescapable that data will be missing. As discussed in Section 2.2, the structure of case law in particular means there will always be significant gaps in the data available. Because courts are designed to decide difficult and high conflict issues, court data is missing much of the record of disputes in society as a whole. Access to the documents in court files helps expand the data available beyond what was finally decided by a judge, but they over represent certain kinds of issues, particularly complex matters involving rich people.

Beyond these concerns, by definition no dataset can be complete. Some of the data is known to be missing — such as court cases under publication bans. Other types of missing data are less obvious. One of the most important categories of missing data is not knowing what outcomes would have been in another circumstances. What would the outcome have been:

- With other lawyers representing the parties?
- If the parties had different identities?
- With a different legislative regime?

This missing data makes it difficult to evaluate outcomes' causes.

It is also difficult to measure many aspects of the world that we want to know about, so instead we develop proxies for what we really want to know (Hand 2020) like billable hours or arrest statistics. They do not measure the actual contribution of a lawyer to a firm's profitability or crime levels in communities, but they present easily counted metrics that can be used instead. This can lead to gaming the system: lawyers are encouraged to take longer on tasks than they otherwise might, and as time can be written off or clients refuse to pay, hours worked are not directly correlated to revenue. In fact, analysis has found that they can be quite removed from each other (Clio 2019).

Another important issue is whether it is possible to extrapolate beyond available data. Any set of data will by necessity have limits in its coverage. It is impossible to know what happened in the past before data was recorded, and it is impossible to know what will happen in the future. This is particularly important when dealing with complex human decision making, because people can respond to the findings based on existing data. New judges are called to the bench, governments change after elections, and people learn.

These are just some of the reasons why data may be missing. All these considerations mean that it is important to consider what is not in the data at hand and account for it in research methodology and how much confidence to put in the findings.

6.4 Ambiguity

Beyond the relatively simple issues of access and completeness of data, there are other elements that make the use of legal data complicated due to the nature of law. Human societies are complex, and human language is imprecise:

> Classical logical models may break down in dealing with legal indeterminacy, a common feature of legal reasoning: even when advocates agree on the facts in issue and the rules for deciding a matter, they can still make reasonable arguments for or against a proposition.
>
> (Ashley 2017, 38).

Though many people who look to legal computing as a way forward are unhappy with this imprecision, in some cases it may in fact be an advantage. For example, many people look to smart contracts to increase efficiencies, but as science fiction writer Ken Liu has observed smart contracts will likely never work well in real life for complex matters. Proponents see the inefficacy in the existing environment, but they do not see how the human interaction of bargaining and negotiation between people leaves room for ambiguity which can help make an agreement possible. Programmers want to take the ambiguity out of the process, because that is not how they think (Doctorow, Liu, and Newitz 2020).

That said, there is more ambiguity in legal documents than there needs to be, and research is being done into how to better isolate the ambiguity in law that is advantageous and that which is not. One of the primary drivers of this at the time of writing is rules as code, which aims to better express what is meant in legal documents. Human languages have syntactic ambiguity in their structure, which has no legal purpose, and it may be advantageous to find ways to remove it. At the same time it may be appropriate to identify topics that are too complex to be legally coded, in which case it may be appropriate to indicate that in these cases a test such as "reasonableness" will be applied by human decision makers. The goal is to identify each of these sources of ambiguity and ensure they are used appropriately (Morris 2021). See Section 3.6 for further discussion of ambiguity in the context of data formats.

6.5 Limitations on language processing

As so much currently contemplated legal data research is being done with existing data in the form of free text documents, it is impossible to avoid the limitations of natural human language as a data source. The room for interpretation and ambiguity in human language is significant, and using written documents as source data requires interpretation when it is used for analysis. This is particularly difficult when using language created by people without subject matter expertise in law, as they may not be able to articulate their issues in a structured way.

Search queries are an example of a way that people interact with legal materials, and these datasets could be significant sources of data into how people understand and interact with the law. It seems that legal information retrieval systems, such as research platforms, should be able to interpret queries in the ways people intend, but so far there is generally no way to accomplish this (Ashley 2017, 316). The disconnect between human beings' intentions and the literal nature of computers' programming means that there continue to be limitations on what systems can do:

> Algorithms do exactly what they are programmed to do, which sometimes creates a problem for programmers. . . . Right now machines will deliver you exactly what you wish for — and we're not capable yet of wishing for the right thing. We can certainly use algorithms to supplement our thinking but knowing what's ahead still requires people who can listen, analyze, and make connections.
>
> (Webb 2016, 91)

While researchers have had some success in categorizing the writing of legal experts, they have had much less with non-experts. Analysis of self represented parties looking to make claims against their lawyers to the American Bar Association found that their descriptions of the facts and issues of their cases were organized in such a way that attempts to predict outcomes was only slightly better than random assignment (Branting et al. 2020). It is possible that automated means will never be sufficient to analyze this kind of writing.

That said, there are also issues with analyzing experts' writing. For example, it is an important problem in legal artificial intelligence to be able to discern whether judges believe the assertions they make to be true — many times they are simply stating the positions of the parties (Ashley 2017, 369). These kinds of complexities will need to be addressed for the creation of fully functioning systems able to use existing legal content in the ways many anticipate.

As decision making applications become more sophisticated, there are anticipated to be problems because computer programs can apply classical logical deduction to problems, but they cannot support arguing both for and against a proposition, which makes them inadequate for modeling legal arguments (Ashley 2017, 128). Inferences also change once information is added or becomes invalid. When dealing with law in particular, it is important to consider that "Legal claims need not be 'true'; they only need to satisfy a given proof standard" (Ashley 2017, 129).

6.6 Sampling

Sampling is the process of collecting and selecting what data points will be included in analysis. In most situations, it is not feasible to analyze full datasets, so a sample is selected to stand in for the whole. Statistical analysis requires adequate sampling to be reliable. The sample size and attributes are selected based on considerations like how confident researchers want to be in their results, but one of the most important elements of a sample is that it must be a random set of points from the complete underlying dataset. Legal datasets tend not to have this structure, because the recorded data does not include all the possible points, and the points that are included are not randomly distributed. Instead they are selected by people according to their own preference or according to various rules: "Sometimes the data contain features that, for spurious reasons such as coincidence or biased selection, happen to the associated with the outcomes of cases in a particular collection" (Ashley 2017, 111). Matters are usually selected for inclusion in the written case law in particular based on attributes of the data. The most common criteria used for recording matters is that they are unusual, because legal systems focus on defining ranges of possible outcomes, or that the parties have extensive resources.

Analytics and sample size

One major issue with legal data for machine learning applications in particular is the small sample sizes available for many datasets. While there were approximately 120,000 intellectual property cases in the United States over the ten year period leading up to 2006 (Walker 2019, 121), but over the same period a dataset for the Supreme Court of Canada would include approximately 1000 cases. These numbers quickly become quite small if they are further parsed to reflect only particular areas of law or individual adjudicators, lawyers, or parties. There are few datasets internationally that are as large as the American intellectual property corpus.

It is difficult to run machine learning on such small numbers of documents. Researchers looking at a set of decisions issued by the Singapore Supreme Court found that there were 6,227 decisions issued between 2000 and 2019. However, when they examined how to run machine learning over the data found that some techniques such as using pre-trained language models as opposed to task specific language models were quite effective (Soh, Lim, and Chai 2019).

These kinds of techniques will be necessary if machine learning and other techniques are going to be used in smaller jurisdictions and with topics that have lower case volumes. This is important, because narrowing analytics applications to particular areas of law is one of the ways that it can be effective. It is easier to analyze decision making in a narrow and discrete areas of the law, like bail or refugee hearings, than something broad like commercial disputes or other heterogeneous matters (McGill and Salyzyn 2021).

6.7 Cost

It remains to be seen how effective applications using legal data will be, but there is hope that they will be the source of needed change. However, there are real worries that even if data driven applications are useful, the cost of setting them up, especially the cost of creating adequate data to build them with, will be prohibitively expensive. That said, the legal services market in the United States alone is forecast to be worth $767.1 billion USD in 2021 (Statista Research Department n.d.), which does not include the value for the portion of the legal system provided by others, such as the government and non-profit groups.

> "There are numerous ways that artificial intelligence and machine learning could improve the service sector, but that improvement will result in systems that are more costly than current ones. AI advances are fueled by data, and data-gathering done well is expensive." (Pasquale 2020, 197)

These values imply that significant gains can be made at the system level, and that they would have the potential to offset substantial investment in productivity improvements. However, these amounts are spread over large numbers of organizations and jurisdictions, many of which will not be able to share solutions. To get some idea of how much difference productivity gains can make, consider that at one time computers were so expensive that only large institutions and governments could have them. Now they can be added to household devices like thermostats and pregnancy tests that are cost competitive with similar non-digital products, but these kinds of price changes are considerably less likely in law, especially in the short to medium terms.

6.8 Jurisdiction

It is clear that there will continue to be differences in how the law is made available in different jurisdictions, and this will ensure that there will continue to be different research patterns based on geography in addition to the differences people bring to this process through culture and legal traditions. Governments internationally make different decisions based on local laws, priorities, and resource levels.

> While industry and researchers have not clarified a definition of artificial intelligence, governments internationally are starting to do so. Proposed harmonized regulations for artificial intelligence in the European Union published in April of 2021 define it as follows:
>
> - Machine learning approaches, including supervised, unsupervised and reinforcement learning, using a wide variety of methods including deep learning;
> - Logic- and knowledge-based approaches, including knowledge representation, inductive (logic) programming, knowledge bases, inference and deductive engines, (symbolic) reasoning and expert systems;
> - Statistical approaches, Bayesian estimation, search and optimization methods. (European Commission 2021)

Jurisdiction is one of the most difficult to navigate elements in any system that aims to run computing on the law. For example, the hardest part of the development of applications to do relatively simple things like developing a website to sell airline tickets is to make it work across all jurisdictions and not break the process or the law where there are different regulatory requirements (Finley 2018). Different jurisdictions have diverse issues and priorities that arise from issues like local laws, politics, economics, and technological development.

6.9 Structure

The facts that many data points in law are missing or not recorded and that the points which are included tend to be selected systematically means that statistical analysis techniques cannot give reliable results for many outcomes. This is especially true for analyses that aim to describe the experiences of complete populations, such as all the people in a population whose marriages dissolve or who have interactions with the criminal justice system. It works better for populations that are better represented in the data, for example looking at Supreme Court of the United States written decisions as a data source to understand possible outcomes for appeals to the Court. This is because matters that are appealed to the Supreme Court are significantly more likely to be represented in written decisions. A discussion of different types of data and common issues with them follows.

Case law

Case law is one of the most commonly analyzed sources of data in the legal space. This is understandable, as it has several attributes that make it appealing:

- It is publicly available
- It has defined inputs and outcomes
- The stakes in these proceedings are high, both personally and financially

That said, there are significant issues with the use of case law as a dataset for analysis.

> "When you see a case as a data point you can dehumanize the participants." (Philip Chung)

The first issue with case law that makes it difficult to analyze is that it is mainly in free text and only semi-structured. This means that while most written decisions have certain sections like spaces for parties', lawyers', and judges' names, and docket numbers, judges have significant discretion in how they are composed. This has created challenges for those who seek to analyze them, as significant work needs to be done to parse them into analyzable formats. This is likely to be a surmountable problem with sufficient care and investment and as free text analysis improves over time.

Though they can run to hundreds of pages, court decisions are relatively lacking in detail, especially considering how complex disputes in the world can be. This can be improved if docket data is also available, but court data is limited because the majority of matters relating to legal issues do not go to court at all. Anything that settles out of court will not have a public record of the result, and, even where matters do go to court, routine matters often do not have written judgements. Instead, many decisions are issued orally, and even decisions with significant public importance may or may not be written down and distributed (Hoadley 2018). This has also been an issue for access to law in South Africa where court transcripts are provided through a commercial services, which require payment for the documents before they can be published (Pillay 2021).

Analysis shows that publication bias means that the corpus of published court judgements is biased in a way that "reflects judicial attributes and not merely case characteristics" (Carlson, Livermore, and Rockmore 2020, 227). This limits researchers' ability to infer causal relationships and outcomes. There are several ways case and judicial attributes can affect publication of case law:

- Issues in cases may be common and create no new law
- Judges may prioritize particular kinds of matters to spend more time on
- There may be cost concerns, including time scarcity for writing

- There may be concerns about avoiding potential conflict with other judges
- There may be risk of scrutiny by higher courts (Carlson, Livermore, and Rockmore 2020, 232)

These issues mean that the use of case law as source material for quantitative analysis needs to be carefully considered before it can be done with confidence. In the past, most of this work was done with the intention of proving that this kind of analysis can be done. Now it is becoming integrated into practice and decision making in communities, and it is important that it be done correctly without making claims that are not valid. At the time of writing, there is a research project being carried out at Oxford University to assess if case law is suitable for use as data to feed into artificial intelligence applications (Winterton 2021). It will be interesting to see what is found.

Legislation

To date legislation is a less popular source of data for analysis than case law. This may be because of the way it behaves in society: there are less frequent outcomes with such important effects for individuals and society with legislation than there are in court decisions. However, legislation does change regularly. It can be passed, challenged, interpreted, and amended, but it is not as lively as case law. That said, there are many opportunities for analysis. In addition to interpretation by the courts, statutory rules are also given additional detail through secondary legislation or regulations, which are written by organizations that legislation delegates the authority to, such as government departments.

Particular issues are frequently affected by multiple pieces of legislation. These networks of documents, which are generally connected by direct citation networks or implied references, are essential to understand when using legislation as a data source.

Superficially, legislation is intended to be a clear set of rules to be implemented, but in practice written rules are often more open to challenge than drafters intend. Intended or not, legislation is broadly open to interpretation:

> Semantic ambiguity and vagueness are concessions to human, social, and political reality. The legislature cannot fashion language sufficiently detailed to anticipate all of the situations it may wish to regulate. Instead it employs more general terminology in statutory rules and relies on the courts to interpret and apply the abstract terms and concepts in new fact situations.
>
> (Ashley 2017)

This has led to calls to write legislation as code, so that it is more comprehensible and useful in computing applications. Whether the governance of human societies will prove to be conducive to being expressed as code in practice, which some see as a desire to reduce important elements of human societies to a series of complex if-then statements, remains to be seen. However, it seems likely that the many powerful players in the legal space may resist changes to their processes, and legal traditions like judicial independence will have significant impacts on the outcomes of these trends.

At the present time, legislation is generally not written with a process that produces a coherent set of rules that can be understood as a code or system in common law countries. Instead, it is a series of documents with multiple edits made over many years that have been made to address particular political concerns and societal needs of the day.

A notable exception to this ethos of legislation drafting is civil codes, which are designed to provide full statements of the law with less influence from the courts. Nevertheless, they frequently have complex networks of citations which can be used to help understand the process of their creation (Badawi and Dari-Mattiacci 2019). Civil law jurisdictions' case law has been observed to be converging in some ways with that from common law jurisdictions (Beauchamp-Tremblay and Dusséaux 2019).

Because the issues surrounding the publication of legislation, such as privacy, are less contentious than case law, it may be a fruitful area of law to explore for future analysis.

Law firms' data

Well used proprietary data is a potential source of competitive advantage that law firms can use to differentiate themselves. Purchased or subscribed content and applications are not unique, and the expertise of the people who work in a firm can leave with those people if they go. The content they create and insights into the processes they follow to do so, in contrast, can be used in many ways:

- To generate valuable tools that can provide value to clients
- To better development opportunities for new employees
- To support potential commercial opportunities if developed for use by people outside the firm

That said, there are likely to be significant issues with any source of data that is created by a large number of people with little training in data standards, and who do not consider creating the data to be their primary role. For example, law firms' client files are an incomplete data aggregation. Documents may be missing, because of issues like emails not being filed properly, and there are frequently multiple copies of particular document, with no easy way to know which is the final one.

Over time, many firms have had projects to create tools based on internally generated documents, like databases of research memos. There have also been projects that use firms' documents as foundations for commercial publishing products, after sufficiently isolating client specific data. These kinds of projects typically use data in essentially anecdotal ways, and they do not require statistical validity.

Given current developments in the technology available, especially natural language processing and law firm management software, there are other possible applications for firm data, such as:

- Systems to parse how likely a particular matter is to be successful for the firm
- Creating flow charts with likelihoods of particular events and outcomes and assigning dollar values for potential costs and awards
- Evaluating the revenue and profitability of particular practice areas, lawyers, and clients

These kinds of applications have the potential to be valuable, but they will be difficult to verify statistically. They also have the potential to drive critical business decisions that may give unfair or unprofitable recommendations if they are used without caution. Quantitative recommendations often have an air of more certainty than they should have, so it is important for firms to evaluate the quality of the data before making mission critical decisions based on them.

6.10 Risks

There are many possible risks arising from increased used of analytics in law and the changes it will bring to the practice of law and governance. Some of them are more immediate than others, such as the unjust outcomes for people of different races found in the outcome patterns for bail recommendation software (Angwin et al. 2016). Some are more abstract — it has been suggested that machine learning applications may lead to the deskilling of lawyers. As computer systems improve their ability to simulate the skills of the human beings who train them, the domain experts will gradually lose skill as they rely on the assists instead of doing the work themselves (Hildebrandt 2017, 14). Some law schools in the United States in particular have started integrating courses on data and the law into their curricula in efforts to better prepare students for the future of practice that will integrate more data driven tools and need to reflect better understanding of how data can be used to assess circumstances like potential instances of injustice (Nayyer 2021).

Mireille Hildebrandt lists the following issues with the increased adoption of artificial intelligence in law:

(1) opacity of the ML [machine learning] software may render decisions based on its output inscrutable and thereby incontestable; (2) the shift from meaningful information to computation entails a shift from reason to

statistics, and from argumentation to simulation; (3) in the process of developing and testing data driven legal intelligence a set of fundamental rights may be infringed, compromised or even violated, and notably the right to privacy, to nondiscrimination, to the presumption of innocence due process, while also impacting consumer and employee protection and competition law. Finally . . . (4) to the extent that the algorithms become highly efficient due to being trained by excellent domain experts in law — lawyers may outsource part of their work, as a result of which they may deskill. (Hildebrandt 2017, 11–12)

Some of these risks are integrated into the regulatory system, including such concepts as innovation risks. There are two main dimensions to innovation risks in machine learning in law. This first is "blocking risk" as data may be controlled by intellectual property rights or data protection laws. The second is "over regulation", which may inhibit the development of artificial intelligence due to significant regulatory costs. These concerns require "calibrating the regulatory burden" based on need (Hacker 2020, 4).

Some of the risks associated with using data analytics in law are not technical at all. Instead they come from the ways people organize their societies, governments, and organizations. Thinking about these limitations critically is crucial to understanding how the use of data can be integrated into legal systems and bring anticipated benefits.

One of the major sources of issues with legal data is that often it is not available in formats that will support analysis, and, even when it is available, it frequently has significant biases due to the way it was created. The documents that record legal processes are usually not created with the intention that they would be used systematically as data at all. Instead, they are created to document the result of events that the creators understood to be distinct to a particular set of facts, such as a court case. This can make it difficult to analyze it in the ways other data is analyzed. There are many examples of artificial intelligence systems that use inappropriate data to assess outcomes, for example, a medical triaging artificial intelligence system that identified patients for new treatment was 50% less likely to recommend it for black patients. This was because it used cost of care as a proxy for severity of illness. When they removed the cost of care metric from this system the bias was removed (Obermeyer et al. 2019). However not all bias may be discovered or remedied so easily.

6.11 Conclusion

There are concerns about resistance to the use of data based applications in law and how the culture of law is limiting the potential for improvements. Many of these are specious, but there are legitimate concerns. For example, Joshua Walker has observed that many lawyers do not like to see outcomes in probabiliistic terms because a person cannot be 79% guilty of murder (Walker 2019, 214). Another important concern is that computing systems as they are being developed and applied now lack a sense of the history of what they are analyzing (Pasquale 2021), with systems as dynamic and high stakes as law this will be an insurmountable obstacle until it is solved. This is not to say that ideas for innovation should be censored before they can be fleshed out or evaluated because their impact cannot easily be measured. It is important not to lose sight of qualitative outcomes when looking at quantitative data, but quantitative observations have the potential to provide insights that qualitative observations cannot. The next chapter will discuss some issues particular to artificial intelligence and how it is likely to affect law.

Works cited

Angwin, Julia, Jeff Larson, Surya Mattu, and Lauren Kirchner. 2016. "Machine Bias." *ProPublica*. https://www.propublica.org/article/machine-bias-risk-assessments-in-crim inal-sentencing.

Artificial Lawyer. 2019. "France Bans Judge Analytics, 5 Years in Prison for Rule Breakers." *Artificial Lawyer* (blog). June 4, 2019. https://www.artificiallawyer.com/ 2019/06/04/france-bans-judge-analytics-5-years-in-prison-for-rule-breakers/.

Ashley, Kevin D. 2017. *Artificial Intelligence and Legal Analytics: New Tools for Law Practice in the Digital Age*. Cambridge: Cambridge University Press.

Badawi, Adam B., and Giuseppe Dari-Mattiacci. 2019. "Reference Networks and Civil Codes." In *Law as Data: Computation, Text, and the Future of Legal Analysis*, 339–365. The SFI Press Seminar Series. Santa Fe: The SFI Press.

Beauchamp-Tremblay, Xavier, and Antoine Dusséaux. 2019. "Not Your Grandparents' Civil Law: Decisions Are Getting Longer. Why and What Does It Mean in France and Québec?" *Slaw* (blog). June 20, 2019. http://www.slaw.ca/2019/06/20/not-your-gra ndparents-civil-law-decisions-are-getting-longer-why-and-what-does-it-mean-in-fra nce-and-quebec/.

Branting, Karl, Carlos Balhana, Craig Pfeifer, John Aberdeen, and Bradford Brown. 2020. "Judges Are from Mars, Pro Se Litigants Are from Venus: Predicting Decisions from Lay Text." In *Frontiers in Artificial Intelligence and Applications*, edited by Serena Villata, Jakub Harašta, and Petr Křemen, 215–218. IOS Press. https://doi.org/ 10.3233/FAIA200867.

Carlson, Keith, Michael A. Livermore, and Daniel N. Rockmore. 2020. "The Problem of Data Bias in the Pool of Published U.S. Appellate Court Opinions." *Journal of Empirical Legal Studies* 17 (2): 224–261. https://doi.org/10.1111/jels.12253.

Clio. 2019. "2019 Legal Trends Report." Burnaby, Canada: Clio. https://www.clio.com/ resources/legal-trends/2019-report/read-online/.

Doctorow, Cory, Ken Liu, and Annalee Newitz. 2020. "Cory Doctorow – Tech in Sci-Fi & ATTACK SURFACE w/ Ken Liu & Annalee Newitz." Virtual, October 20. https:// www.youtube.com/watch?v=0LHCLd1FvLw.

European Commission. 2021. "Annexes to the Proposal for a Regulation of the European Parliament and of the Council Laying Down Harmonised Rules on Artificial

Intelligence (Artificial Intelligence Act) and Amending Certain Union Legislative Acts." COM(2021) 206 final. Brussels: European Commission.

Finley, Klint. 2018. "How Software Code Could Help You Grapple with the Legal Code." *Wired*, 2018. https://www.wired.com/story/how-software-code-help-grapple-with-legal-code/.

Georgia et al. v. Public.Resource.Org, Inc. 2020. Supreme Court of the United States.

Hacker, Philipp. 2020. "A Legal Framework for AI Training Data." SSRN Scholarly Paper ID 3556598. Rochester, NY: Social Science Research Network. https://doi.org/10.2139/ssrn.3556598.

Hand, David J. 2020. *Dark Data: Why What You Don't Know Matters*. Princeton: Princeton University Press.

Heaven, Will Douglas. 2020. "AI Is Wrestling with a Replication Crisis." *MIT Technology Review* (blog). November 12, 2020. https://www.technologyreview.com/2020/11/12/1011944/artificial-intelligence-replication-crisis-science-big-tech-google-deepmind-facebook-openai/.

Hildebrandt, Mireille. 2017. "Law As Computation in the Era of Artificial Legal Intelligence. Speaking Law to the Power of Statistics." SSRN Scholarly Paper ID 2983045. Rochester, NY: Social Science Research Network. https://doi.org/10.2139/ssrn.2983045.

Hoadley, Daniel. 2018. "Open Access to Case Law —How Do We Get There?" *Internet Newsletter for Lawyers* (blog). November 23, 2018. https://www.infolaw.co.uk/newsletter/2018/11/open-access-case-law-get/.

Légifrance. 2019. "Article 33 — LOI N° 2019–222 Du 23 Mars 2019 de Programmation 2018–2022 et de Réforme Pour La Justice (1)." Légifrance. March 24, 2019. https://www.legifrance.gouv.fr/eli/loi/2019/3/23/JUST1806695L/jo/article_33.

McGill, Jena, and Amy Salyzyn. 2021. "Judging by Numbers: How Will Judicial Analytics Impact the Justice System and Its Stakeholders?" *Dalhousie Law Journal* 44 (1): (Forthcoming).

Morris, Jason. 2021. (Principal Research Engineer, Symbolic Artificial Intelligence for the Singapore Management University Centre for Computational Law), in discussion with the author.

Nayyer, Kim. 2021. (Edward Cornell Law Librarian, Associate Dean for Library Services, and Professor of the Practice at Cornell University), in discussion with the author.

Obermeyer, Ziad, Brian Powers, Christine Vogeli, and Sendhil Mullainathan. 2019. "Dissecting Racial Bias in an Algorithm Used to Manage the Health of Populations." *Science* 366 (6464): 447–453. https://doi.org/10.1126/science.aax2342.

Pasquale, Frank. 2020. *New Laws of Robotics: Defending Human Expertise in the Age of AI*. Belknap Press: An Imprint of Harvard University Press. https://www.amazon.ca/New-Laws-Robotics-Defending-Expertise/dp/0674975227.

Pasquale, Frank. 2021. "*Battle of the Experts: The Promise and Peril of Automating Knowledge Work.*" Presented at the 2021 Canadian Association of Law Libraries Virtual Conference, Virtual, June 2.

Pillay, Carina. 2021. (Project Director SAFLII [Southern African Legal Information Institute]), in discussion with the author.

Soh, Jerrold, How Khang Lim, and Ian Ernst Chai. 2019. "Legal Area Classification: A Comparative Study of Text Classifiers on Singapore Supreme Court Judgments." In *Proceedings of the Natural Legal Language Processing Workshop 2019*, 67–77.

Minneapolis, Minnesota: Association for Computational Linguistics. https://doi.org/10.18653/v1/W19-2208.

Statista Research Department. n.d. "Size of the Global Legal Services Market 2015–2023." Statista. Accessed March 21, 2021. https://www.statista.com/statistics/605125/size-of-the-global-legal-services-market/.

Vivekanandan, V.C. 2021. (Vice Chancellor at Hidayatullah National Law University), in discussion with the author.

Walker, Joshua. 2019. *On Legal AI*. Washington, DC: Full Court Press.

Webb, Amy. 2016. *The Signals Are Talking: Why Today's Fringe Is Tomorrow's Mainstream*. New York: PublicAffairs.

Winterton, Jules. 2021. (Chief Executive Officer, British and Irish Legal Information Institute (BAILII)), in discussion with the author.

Chapter 7

Artificial intelligence

7.1 Introduction

In recent years, there has been a great deal of hype on the use of artificial intelligence in law, and it seems clear there is room for optimism. Artificial intelligence technologies will support new legal applications that will take over many tasks people find tedious, and lawyers' clients are likely to benefit from getting more services for lower fees. Artificial intelligence will also create new opportunities for research about and understanding of the law and legal system.

However, this outlook is paired with concerns that existing business models will be disrupted, and that the implications for society are not clear. More worryingly, these systems may not be accessible in a way that will allow verification of inputs and results, since many artificial intelligence developers treat their work as trade secrets, and users may not have the expertise or ability to audit the results. The legal community needs to be sophisticated in knowing how to evaluate claims associated with these developments.

The most commonly discussed applications of artificial intelligence in law are in legal practice, with repetitive and routine work being seen to be particularly likely to be automated. Some of the work that is already being done by artificial intelligence applications include applications in electronic discovery, legal research, transcription, form completion, and document creation. Beyond this, there are considerable potential opportunities to apply artificial intelligence to making systems more efficient or fair.

7.2 Definition

Before discussing the impacts people anticipate will come from developments in legal artificial intelligence, it is valuable to spend time discussing what artificial intelligence, and more specifically legal artificial intelligence, is. At its most basic artificial intelligence is the use of computing applications to do tasks that are usually done using human intelligence. The term is generally used to describe functions that are still novel enough to surprise people: once the applications become mundane they are not called artificial intelligence any longer.

DOI: 10.4324/9781003127307-7

This gives room for the shifting of definitions, and it has given the phrase "artificial intelligence" a longer life span than many other terms used to describe new technologies. The kinds of tasks identified as artificial intelligence change over time because we adjust what we include when we get used to new possibilities. The artificial intelligence of ten or twenty years ago has become accepted as normal functionality for computers now.

> Artificial intelligence is technology that is always just beyond or just within reach.

There are two things that can be defined as legal artificial intelligence. The first is the use of artificial intelligence in legal processes, including things like analytical methods, decision support, or practice improvement. The second definition of legal artificial intelligence is artificial intelligence that is legally compliant, as opposed to artificial intelligence which is illegal (Walker 2019, 69). Both of these are important, but this book is primarily interested in the former.

7.3 Promise and limits

There are many legal applications that have automated tasks that require considerable human effort and many more that will come in the future. There are also applications that have and will continue to make tasks possible that would not be feasible at all without advanced computing. These developments will continue to lead to opportunities that did not exist before. Much of this new capability is not particularly novel from a basic research perspective. Rather, developing techniques for deployment of these discoveries and exploration of use cases is what is of primary interest.

This means that existing applications of artificial intelligence tend to be applications of principles like linear regression or to extract metadata from document sets (Walters 2021). Many researchers and developers believe that general artificial intelligence, or a system that can be applied to varied new situations without extensive reprogramming or training, is the goal of research in this field. However, it is not possible to simply continue to add more data to a system until general artificial intelligence develops (Soh 2021).

> "There is nothing inherently novel or difficult about splitting a dataset into training and test sets and performing model assessments. . . . . The advantage brought by machine learning techniques comes from the fact that computational power now allows us to quickly estimate complicated models and assess their quality repeatedly." (Copus, Hübert, and Laqueur 2019, 34)

There are many limitations to what artificial intelligence is likely to accomplish in the immediate future and a smaller number of limitations on what artificial intelligence will likely ever be able to do. It is probable that these applications will continue to require supervision, and that moving from tools capable of assisting people in their tasks to full automation will be difficult.

Consider self driving cars, there is significant difference in the development effort required to make a car capable of self driving most of the time and capable of self driving all of the time. This divide will make it difficult to develop self driving cars for the consumer market, because a car that is self driving most of the time, but which suddenly gives the human occupant control when something unexpected happens will not be safe, especially as people become less used to driving (Fry 2018, 136).

It may be that a better model is to consider centaur chess, a combination of a human player and artificial intelligence playing chess in tandem. The artificial intelligence identifies possible moves and outcomes, while the human player selects the strategy knowing that nothing has been missed (Fry 2018, 202). Requiring the involvement of a person in the implementation of artificial intelligence may not protect existing business models and organizations from impacts. Instead it is possible that the future of law in an artificial intelligence intensive environment will look like accounting before and after the adoption of spreadsheet software: some things will be automated, but the difficult tasks will be carried out by people (Morris 2021).

7.4 Types of artificial intelligence

To understand the use of artificial intelligence it will help to understand the main types of application usually grouped in this category:

- The first type runs complex statistical analyses and makes inferences and predictions based on input data. It is based on past activity and has assumptions that can be played with to explore different ways of describing existing patterns in order to describe patterns in outcomes. It works better with structured data.
- The second type, machine learning, uses computer programs to run over data and draw their own conclusions. The input data can be in different formats including numerical and textual sources. This type is referred to as "self learning" and requires less data than statistical analyses.
- The third type of artificial intelligence to consider is vaporware. Vapor ware is products that are presented as being powered by artificial intelligence, but are in fact built on human work. These products are often in earlier stages of development, and having people do the work allows them to be available quicker and cheaper than would be possible if the full artificial intelligence system were developed.

Statistical analysis

Some artificial intelligence applications are essentially complex statistical tools. They can be run over very large datasets and make predictions about outcomes based on existing behavior. One of the main commercial applications for this kind of tool is predicting purchase decision on online commerce sites. These tools are being used to generate statistical analyses of the outcomes of trials or to look at the relative success of lawyers in different types of matters. To give some idea of the scale of data required, predicting whether a customer will buy a product on an online sales platform generally requires the customer to interact with the site at least fifty times per month. This works out to 600 data points per year and is predicting relatively simple decisions.

There has been some success in predicting court outcomes using this technique (Katz, Bommarito, II, and Blackman 2017; Walker 2019), but it is debatable whether there is sufficient data in many types of court matters and most jurisdictions to provide suitable data for this kind of analysis. This is especially the case in smaller jurisdictions where there are fewer court cases. It is common for those carrying out this kind of analysis to point out that these techniques describe existing patterns in the data, and that they should not be used to predict future outcomes.

The basis for many of these analyses is regression. A regression line is a line that is drawn using a series of data points to guide it and will aim to generate the best fit using the data available. Computers can use significantly more complicated calculations to find regression lines in more complex data using a larger number of data points. The regression line identifies the trend, which can then be used to make observations on new matters based on the existing data.

Machine learning

In contrast with applications based on statistics, machine learning applications use programs to run over data looking for patterns. Machine learning requires significantly less data to support it, and it can use both numerical and textual data. It uses cues in the data to find patterns.

There are many issues identified with machine learning. Importantly, relationships the algorithms identify to navigate the data may not be categories that are meaningful to us. Machine learning applications do not generally record and share the information that would be required to assess whether the basis for outputs is based on acceptable criteria. For example, researchers have made glasses that look normal to human eyes, but which fool face recognition machine learning algorithms: "Clearly the machines are seeing things we are not, and equally clearly, those things do not represent the aspect we are interested in." (Hand 2020, 303)

The difficulty associated with identifying why machine learning algorithms give the outputs they do is particularly concerning in the context of law where structured decision making and concerns like evidence rules are so central to process. It is unclear if legal cultures that value logical decision making and review will change to accept the outputs of black boxes, or if machine learning applications will be developed that are more amenable to oversight. There may also be compromises between human rules and the limitations of these technologies, and these requirements may be adjusted to an acceptable balance.

Vaporware

There is a third kind of artificial intelligence application that is frequently advertised, which can be described as "vaporware". Vapor ware is applications that have either been announced or made available for sale but are not yet fully functional as artificial intelligence applications. It is often systems that seem to run on artificial intelligence technologies, but which in fact do not. Instead, they are frequently built by people manually adding the content that the artificial intelligence application is supposed to be processing. This is frequently done because initially it is cheaper to pay people to add this content than it is to develop full artificial intelligence capabilities and populate the data.

Vaporware can be used for many reasons. Sometimes a product may start to be sold before it is fully developed. Taking a vaporware product to market means developers can validate ideas with customers before investing the amounts required to build a full application, allowing for more flexibility in development and for more time to build data. The data used in the vaporware product can also be used to feed the artificial intelligence applications as they are developed.

It may not be bad that this is happening: there is nothing wrong in using vaporware as a stage in developing an application. Just understand that there are limits to what can be done with artificial intelligence, and if it sounds too good to be true, it may well be. Vaporware may never be developed into the promised applications. Selling a product before it is ready to do a full task using artificial intelligence can be managed by having people review the generated work product. In fact, some products may never be viable without human review of the outcomes.

Vaporware is likely to continue to be a feature of artificial intelligence systems in law, if only because there are so many new laws or laws that have not been extensively litigated. In these situations, there will likely continue to be a lack of training data, so human expertise will continue to be required. Though the possibility of increased adoption of machine readable law may help alleviate this issue.

Beyond the possibility of dishonesty in selling products based on systems that do not exist. There can also be issues with ethics relating to the ghost work that go into artificial intelligence systems. Where artificial intelligence is not automated, the conditions of the people doing the work can be exploitative (Hao 2020). These issues will likely continue to be important and become more actively discussed as these systems continue to be developed and adopted in law and other sectors.

7.5 Process

> "data is so central to any artificial intelligence system. *Controlling data inputs may be tantamount to controlling the AI output.*" (Walker 2019, 71)

Without discussing the details of setting up artificial intelligence systems, it is useful to understand how legal data is used in this process. Data is used to train artificial intelligence, and it is important to select it carefully. Setting up these systems to handle legal information is more complex than is often anticipated. It took the team developing Kira over two years instead of the original estimate of four months to identify concepts like non-compete contract clauses, and even then the system required manual review (Lohr 2017).

The data used for development of artificial intelligence systems should be as extensive and exhaustive as possible. This is of particular concern because of issues with the sources of data for legal matters. Training data should not reflect only a subset of instances, such as court cases where parties litigated to the end and did not settle, without considering what that means for the outcomes. The law is also dynamic, and it may not be suitable to include the data from before legislative changes or important court decisions as part of a training set.

Assuming there is suitable data to train the application, the next step is to separate the data into segments. These will be used to train the system and then to test it. It is important to plan for how the system will get further feedback as it starts being used. An artificial intelligence system should be improved on an ongoing basis. However, while it is an advantage that these systems can learn from interactions with the systems without extensive intervention, it is dangerous to deploy a system that is continuously learning as a production system because these systems are unpredictable. Legal systems in particular should be verified before they are made available for use (Chatila 2020).

7.6 Likely impacts

In their article "The Great Disruption: How Machine Intelligence Will Transform the Role of Lawyers in the Delivery of Legal Services" John McGinnis and Russell Pearce discuss how different groups of lawyers are likely to be affected by the changes artificial intelligence is bringing. One group that are likely to be helped by artificial intelligence are superstars who will be more recognizable and who will have the ability to extend their reach as artificial intelligence allows them to do more for more people. Another group that will likely benefit is lawyers who are flexible and who can use lower cost inputs to serve middle class and small business clients. While they may not benefit from these changes, there are also lawyers who are likely to be insulated from artificial intelligence impacts, including oral advocates, highly specialized lawyers who practice in areas of law that change frequently, and lawyers who have to persuade clients to do what is in their own best interests. Lawyers who are likely to be most adversely affected are journeyman lawyers who primarily perform routine tasks like writing wills and transferring real estate (McGinnis and Pearce 2019, 3042).

Many companies and organizations have started making artificial intelligence powered applications, and research is ongoing to allow it to better handle more complex tasks. To date, in law these have generally been sold to professional users. There is hope that artificial intelligence will help to democratize legal advice and ameliorate problems like backlogs in courts, but there have been technical and regulatory limitations that have restricted many of them. In certain areas of the law the use of artificial intelligence is maturing, while in others its use is starting to become routine in practice.

Some of the most promising applications in the short to medium term are tools that assist professional users in their work, which avoids some issues because the results are assessed by legal experts who take responsibility for the final work product instead of providing services directly to the public. This has had some impact on the amount of work lawyers are doing in these areas, or more often how long the work takes. Because many law firms use the billable hour business model, this can directly impact their revenues.

Going forward, additional uses of artificial intelligence applications are anticipated, which are forecast to drive efficiency gains. These improvements in productivity are expected to help clients, as they will no longer have to pay as much for these tasks to be completed. However, the outcomes are expected to be more mixed for lawyers, especially if they are not able to change their business models to adjust for these changes.

Other common applications in public facing applications are being developed by legal aid organizations, especially in the United States, in order to find scalable ways of helping people with relatively simple problems. For example, a project started in 2016 by Pro-bono net, Microsoft, and Legal Services Corporation in the United States is working to develop automated systems to perform triage for people looking for legal assistance from legal aid, which will quickly answer questions like who to refer them to and whether they qualify for programs. This application of rules based artificial intelligence is based on data from sources like past cases (Legal Services Corporation n.d., Walters 2021).

It has been proposed that because artificial intelligence is often used to match patterns in human decision making to make decisions in similar situations, the economic impact of artificial intelligence is expected to be primarily felt in a reduction in value placed on routine decision making. Decision making in rare or uncommon situations is another matter: "AI cannot predict what a human would do if that human has never faced a similar situation" (Agrawal, Gans, and Goldfarb 2018, 99). How long it will take for artificial intelligence systems to be comparable to and cost effective against human decision makers remains to be seen.

Machines are and will continue to be bad at predicting rare events. While automating decision making will not eliminate all jobs in law, its economic impact is likely to change them. Consider that a school bus driver might not have to drive an autonomous bus, but someone will still be needed to supervise and protect the children in it (Agrawal, Gans, and Goldfarb 2018, 149). These kinds of changes are difficult to fully anticipate, but they can be expected to be significant.

7.7 Limitations

Much of the discussion about artificial intelligence is still speculation, because the technology and its implementation have not caught up to people's ideas of what might happen. Much of the primary data being used for artificial intelligence in the legal space is free text in the form of written prose, which is drawn from sources like court judgements, legislation, and other legal writing such as commentary or court filings. The ability of artificial intelligence systems to understand complex meaning and extract facts from text is still limited but improving quickly.

These applications are increasingly effective with text the length of paragraphs, and they do well with sentences and phrases. They are rapidly developing the ability to analyze the full text of long documents and draw conclusions regarding what the documents are about. This can be illustrated by thinking about this in relation to machine translation: it is getting better, but it still works segment by segment or sentence by sentence and has limited ability to understand language beyond that level. You cannot run artificial intelligence over text and teach it to speak, but there have been advances in having it compose formal documents like weather reports or legal briefs, and it can start to identify what a document is about.

A great deal of the current discussion about artificial intelligence is driven by marketing hype. In fact when an assessment was made about what technologies were actually being used by artificial intelligence startups in Europe in 2019, 40% did not use artificial intelligence at all (Knight 2019). This is not to say that the long-term outlook for the sector will necessarily be so limited. Taking into consideration technology adoption patterns, it can be anticipated that in the immediate to medium terms the majority of applications will be applied to routine matters with readily available data and these limitations will continue to slow progress toward more complex applications.

7.8 Concerns

There are many concerns associated with the adoption of artificial intelligence, both generally and particularly in relation to law. Here are some of the most commonly discussed topics.

Fairness

One of the most important concerns related to artificial intelligence in law is trying to understand what fairness should look like in these systems. Because many artificial intelligence systems are based on statistics, they can adversely affect some people more than others. Consider the problem of identifying murders in the population: 96% of murderers are male, so more men will be falsely identified if gender is included as a relevant attribute when developing an artificial intelligence system to identify murderers in the population. Following this pattern, for every 100 inaccurately identified potential murders 96 will be men (Fry 2018, 67). This kind of exercise can also then be carried out for other attributes, many of which make it more likely that particular groups of people will be more likely to be targeted.

Taken a step further, research has shown that crimes committed by some groups in some communities are more likely to be observed and acted on than others (O'Neil 2017, 87). This means that not only are members of those groups who are more likely to commit crimes more likely to be unjustly accused, this also applies to members of groups who are more heavily policed. Artificial intelligence applications built using the data associated with these outcomes can be expected to mirror these outcomes. This unfairness is based on available data, and it should not be considered to be an error in the algorithm. Rather, it is naively reflecting human decisions and injustices back at us.

Artificial intelligence systems quickly run into the issue that the way things were decided in the past is not the best way to make decisions in the future. If this technology was adopted in the 1960s, women still would not be going to university much or getting mortgages, and we still would not have diverse lawyers: "Big data processes codify the past. They do not invent the future" (O'Neil 2017, 204). These limitations are compounded in the legal space by the high stakes that can be attached to the way they are used and the nature of the data that is being used to train the systems.

All applications that can be categorized as artificial intelligence involve tradeoffs. They are designed to maximize or minimize certain criteria while ignoring others. Search is one of the most established applications for artificial intelligence, and it is optimized for the benefit of the person searching, and the stakeholders like advertisers on search engines. It is not optimized for the subjects of search. The Right to be Forgotten in the European Union is an example of a regulatory intervention designed to address the interests of these people in a more meaningful way (Pasquale 2020, 105).

Considering what constitutes fairness is essential for successful deployment of these systems. Probability of outcomes for individuals in a particular moment is not the same as probability of outcomes for individuals in society. In a recidivism prediction system the differences in experience leading up to the moment an algorithm is run including differences in experience with policing and the justice system, mean that identical outcomes for people being entered into the application may still not be fair, as the samples of people being considered in the processes are already biased (Wachter-Boettcher 2017, 126).

In cases where artificial intelligence systems make biased recommendations, it can be impossible to know if the bias was intentional, because "no person can trace the steps a program went through to reach its autonomous decisions, as the program maintains no records of these steps." (Etzioni and Etzioni 2016, 139) This is especially an issue with unsupervised machine learning applications, see Sections 3.6 and 4.4 for further discussion of this issue.

Error and bias

There are two primary sources of error or bias in artificial intelligence systems. The first arises when datasets are not adequately sampled, so they do not reflect the full underlying population. This means the insights derived may be mathematically incorrect. There are mathematical ways to try to resolve this issue, but there continues to be the risk that the insights derived will not be correct because only a subset of outcomes is included.

The other main source of error in training artificial intelligence is when the data may represent the full population, but the dataset as a whole is biased. This means that applications built with it may reinforce existing discrimination or unfairness. Consider how important fair results are for situations like justice in hiring, bail decisions, and immigration hearings. This bias is not a mathematical error. There are ways to reduce these errors such as truncating the data by removing dimensions such as gender or race, or adding more dimensions to the system if predicted outcomes are not reflecting the backgrounds of different groups.

For example, in certain artificial intelligence systems it has been identified that people with African ancestry are more likely to have bail denied (Angwin et al. 2016), and women are less likely to be hired for technical roles (Hamilton 2018). By making it clearer that these are different groups with different signals for outcomes, the system may better reflect their situations. It could show that early interactions with police for African Americans are less predictive of reoffending than they are for white offenders, or that women have different backgrounds that point to success when working with technology than men.

Artificial intelligence may also amplify patterns in data. Recommendations for decisions in an artificial intelligence system are more accurately conveyed as probabilities, but a finding that in 70% of cases humans make decisions a certain way may lead to an automated system making recommendations that way 100% of the time. This is an error because this recommendation is in fact 30% wrong. Because these systems' recommendations are probabilities, there will practically always be some error in any binary choice that follows it.

Ethics

Artificial intelligence is a difficult topic because there are simultaneously strong ethical reasons to push forward and to pull back on its adoption. First the push: there are clear access to justice problems around the world, and even people who can afford the legal system are pushing for more reasonable pricing. Artificial intelligence has the potential to drive productivity gains that could help resolve these problems. Then the pull: these technologies are untried, most potential users of the systems do not understand why they work the way they do, and they are difficult to audit or confidently verify.

It may be impossible to be sure where recommendations come from when using machine learning, and it is natural to think that there is an ethical obligation to hesitate in their adoption. In fact, even experts do not know how many artificial intelligence algorithms work at a detailed level. This gives rise to concerns about not knowing what is likely to make them fail, as complex machine-learning approaches could make systems supplying automated decision-making inscrutable (Knight 2017).

The easiest artificial intelligence to justify is applications that provide services to knowledgeable people who can confidently assess the information they are given and use it to make their jobs easier or gain insights they would find difficult to access another way. Some good examples of these kinds of applications include:

- E-discovery
- Search
- Document assembly
- Form filling

Artificial intelligence applications are more difficult to justify when they are based on questionable data or make claims that cannot be supported by the technology or implementation. Bad examples of artificial intelligence include machine learning that affects people's lives in opaque ways without providing adequate opportunities for review.

As artificial intelligence tools are further developed and more widely adopted, it is to be hoped that there will be better ways to assess tools and whether they are appropriate for use. Ideally this will lead to more reliable tools that both members of the legal community and members of the public can use. This may look like advanced artificial intelligence, or it may just look like a thoughtful website with information in plain language and usable forms. There are important things to consider even without considering the overwhelming influence of hype around artificial intelligence. For practicing lawyers is ethical duty:

- Pursuing exhaustiveness in all matters?
- Doing the same things for every client?
- Providing the best value?
- Following clients' preferences?

Predictive analytics have been a particularly fraught topic in discussions about artificial intelligence in law, and there has been a great deal of debate about the ethics of these techniques. While the government of France has outlawed the use of statistical methods on court decisions (Légifrance 2019), big law firms have large in house algorithms that only their clients can access. There needs to be better ways to help people understand likely outcomes of their disputes, and discussion of whether it should be done is likely moot because it is already happening. The question then becomes: who should have access to this important information? So much of the dynamic of law now involves information asymmetry between lawyers and their clients and the general public (Salter 2021).

Many reports say that jobs will disappear, and people will be left behind. By adopting these tools now they may be able to navigate these changes better. One thing that is clear is that we should not be developing experimental artificial intelligence tools to be used on the poorest people who do not have a choice or reasonable access to recourse if they do not get appropriate results. Artificial intelligence applications should be developed for people who have options and who can hire lawyers and appeal decisions if they need them.

7.9 Thinking critically

There are laws that may never be conducive to artificial intelligence methods. For example, European Union non-discrimination law was found to be too "contextual, reliant on intuition, and open to judicial interpretation to be automated" (Wachter, Mittelstadt, and Russell 2020, 1). Artificial intelligence also has a history of over promising and under delivering, resulting in periods of time with little investment in the area in the past, especially from 1974–1980 and 1987–1993, which led to a lack of progress in the field (Walker 2019, 34). It is important to challenge the assertions that artificial intelligence platforms are fit for use and to have a sophisticated understanding of what data is being used to train them.

Some questions to ask yourself to assess whether you are using "artificial intelligence":

1   Does it use large amounts of data across a variety of formats?
2   Does it update the data it uses over time?
3   Does it adapt its decision-making logic over time?
4   Does it adjust for possible biases? (Wade et al. 2020)

There are areas of development in artificial intelligence that are making real progress and some that are not:

- "Genuine rapid progress": perception, such as speech to text and face recognition
- "Imperfect but improving": automated judgement, such as context recognition and spam detection
- "Fundamentally dubious": predicting social outcomes, such as recidivism, job success, or terrorist risk (Narayanan n.d., 10)

As artificial intelligence becomes more integrated into people's work it is not sustainable to develop systems that cannot have particular data elements changed or removed. Instead they must be robust to dynamic changes: it will be desirable to have modularity built into the systems because this will allow a system to be updated without requiring full reprocessing of the data, which means it will not be as brittle (Atkinson 2020). Flexible and externally verified systems with mechanisms for review where appropriate will make the adoption of artificial intelligence significantly more attractive as the technology develops.

7.10 Conclusion

There are promising applications for artificial intelligence in the legal space, and it is to be hoped that people will continue to explore them to make systems work better. However, care needs to be taken in how they are used and sophisticated queries into the technology and what data goes into it. Artificial intelligence driven applications are not reliable without extreme care being taken in their development and selection: "it is easy to lie with artificial intelligence. Most results are extremely sensitive to individual data context and user type. Artificial intelligence platforms are notoriously difficult to benchmark and compare for most commercial contexts." (Walker 2019, 211) The next chapter will discuss the law and politics of legal data and how these external forces are affecting the availability of the data that could be used to develop applications and research in law.

Works cited

Agrawal, Ajay, Joshua Gans, and Avi Goldfarb. 2018. *Prediction Machines: The Simple Economics of Artificial Intelligence*. Boston, Massachusetts: Harvard Business Review Press.

Angwin, Julia, Jeff Larson, Surya Mattu, Lauren Kirchner. 2016. "Machine Bia s." *Pro-Publica*. 2016. https://www.propublica.org/article/machine-bias-risk-assessments-in-criminal-sentencing.

Atkinson, Katie. 2020. "Explainability for AI and Law in the Wild." Presented at the JURIX 2020: 33rd International Conference on Legal Knowledge and Information Systems, Virtual, December 10.

Chatila, Raja. 2020. "Can AI Systems Be Trustworthy?" Presented at the JURIX 2020: 33rd International Conference on Legal Knowledge and Information Systems, Virtual, December 11.

Copus, Ryan, Ryan Hübert, and Hannah Laqueur. 2019. "Big Data, Machine Learning, and the Credibility Revolution in Empirical Legal Studies." In *Law as Data: Computation, Text, and the Future of Legal Analysis*, 21–57. The SFI Press Seminar Series. Santa Fe: The SFI Press.

Etzioni, Amitai, and Oren Etzioni. 2016. "Keeping AI Legal." SSRN Scholarly Paper ID 2726612. Rochester, NY: Social Science Research Network. https://doi.org/10.2139/ssrn.2726612.

Fry, Hannah. 2018. *Hello World: How Algorithms Will Define Our Future and Why We Should Learn to Live with It*. New York, NY: WW Norton.

Hamilton, Isobel Asher. 2018. "Amazon Built AI to Hire People, but It Discriminated Against Women." *Business Insider*. October 10, 2018. https://www.businessinsider. com/amazon-built-ai-to-hire-people-discriminated-against-women-2018-10.

Hand, David J. 2020. *Dark Data: Why What You Don't Know Matters*. Princeton: Princeton University Press.

Hao, Karen. 2020. "The Problems AI Has Today Go Back Centuries." *MIT Technology Review*, July 31, 2020. https://www.technologyreview.com/2020/07/31/1005824/decolo nial-ai-for-everyone/.

Katz, Daniel Martin, Michael J. Bommarito, II, and Josh Blackman. 2017. "A General Approach for Predicting the Behavior of the Supreme Court of the United States." *PLOS ONE* 12 (4): e0174698. https://doi.org/10.1371/journal.pone.0174698.

Knight, Will. 2017. "*The Dark Secret at the Heart of AI.*" *MIT Technology Review*. April 11, 2017. https://www.technologyreview.com/2017/04/11/5113/the-dark-secret-a t-the-heart-of-ai/.

Knight, Will. 2019. "About 40% of Europe's 'AI Companies' Don't Use Any AI at All." *MIT Technology Review*. March 5, 2019. https://www.technologyreview.com/2019/03/ 05/65990/about-40-of-europes-ai-companies-dont-actually-use-any-ai-at-all/.

Legal Services Corporation. n.d. "Simplifying Legal Help." LSC - Legal Services Corporation: America's Partner for Equal Justice. Accessed June 7, 2021. https://www.lsc. gov/node/3500.

Légifrance. 2019. "Article 33 - LOI N° 2019–222 Du 23 Mars 2019 de Programmation 2018–2022 et de Réforme Pour La Justice (1)." Légifrance. March 24, 2019. https:// www.legifrance.gouv.fr/eli/loi/2019/3/23/JUST1806695L/jo/article_33.

Lohr, Steve. 2017. "A.I. Is Doing Legal Work. But It Won't Replace Lawyers, Yet." *The New York Times*, March 19, 2017, sec. Technology. https://www.nytimes.com/2017/ 03/19/technology/lawyers-artificial-intelligence.html.

McGinnis, John O., and Russell G. Pearce. 2019. "The Great Disruption: How Machine Intelligence Will Transform the Role of Lawyers in the Delivery of Legal Services." *Actual Problems of Economics and Law* 13, no. 2 (July 18, 2019). https://doi.org/10. 21202/1993-047X.13.2019.2.1230-1250.

Morris, Jason. 2021. (Principal Research Engineer, Symbolic Artificial Intelligence for the Singapore Management University Centre for Computational Law), in discussion with the author.

Narayanan, Arvind. n.d. "How to Recognize AI Snake Oil." Princeton University Department of Computer Science. Accessed November 14, 2020. https://www.cs.prin ceton.edu/~arvindn/talks/MIT-STS-AI-snakeoil.pdf.

O'Neil, Cathy. 2017. *Weapons of Math Destruction: How Big Data Increases Inequality and Threatens Democracy*. Reprint edition. New York: Broadway Books.

Pasquale, Frank. 2020. *New Laws of Robotics: Defending Human Expertise in the Age of AI*. Cambridge, Massachusetts: Belknap Press of Harvard University Press. https:// www.amazon.ca/New-Laws-Robotics-Defending-Expertise/dp/0674975227.

Salter, Shannon. 2021. (Chair at Civil Resolution Tribunal of British Columbia, and adjunct professor at the UBC Allard School of Law), in discussion with the author.

Soh, Jerrold. 2021. (Assistant Professor of Law and Deputy Director, Centre for Computational Law at the Singapore Management University), in discussion with the author.

Wachter, Sandra, Brent Mittelstadt, and Chris Russell. 2020. "Why Fairness Cannot Be Automated: Bridging the Gap Between EU Non-Discrimination Law and AI." SSRN

Scholarly Paper ID 3547922. Rochester, NY: Social Science Research Network. https://doi.org/10.2139/ssrn.3547922.

Wachter-Boettcher, Sara. 2017. *Technically Wrong: Why Digital Products Are Designed to Fail You*. New York, NY: WW Norton.

Wade, Michael, Amit Joshi, Mark J. Greeven, Robert Hooijberg, and Shlomo Ben-Hur. "How Intelligent Is Your AI?" *MIT Sloan Management Review*, 2020. https://sloanreview.mit.edu/article/how-intelligent-is-your-ai/.

Walker, Joshua. 2019. *On Legal AI*. Washington, DC: Full Court Press.

Walters, Ed. 2021. (CEO at Fastcase), in discussion with the author.

Chapter 8

The law and politics of legal data

8.1 Introduction

Legal data can include many things, and there are certainly politics in organizations like law firms and professional standards for legal providers that affect how data is collected and used, but the topic of most interest from the perspective of law and politics is data associated with primary law. Whether court and legislative data is available or not and in what formats it is published is different around the world. It depends on local policy decisions, laws, and histories.

It is not possible to extricate the creation and use of data about the law from the process requirements associated with it. In early 2021, the government of Washington, D.C. was unable to pass legislation, because rules intended to allow Congress to oversee the city required the delivery of hard copies of bills before they become law. After the insurrection on January 6, fences were put around the Capital Building and these bills could not be delivered, so the last step to bring them into force could not be completed (Lefrak 2021).

Having legal documents available for use as data requires extensive levels of investment in publishing and infrastructure. Existing levels of investment vary greatly by jurisdiction depending on decisions governments or other organizations make, and what resources are available to deploy to ensure that legal documents are published in a way that supports various uses. In addition to these technological requirements, there are also extensive policy and legal issues that affect whether legal data is accessible and in what formats.

Beyond these requirements, law is different from many other data sources, because it is constantly growing and changing. It has complex rules about whether particular rules are in effect, which are not directly dependent on time. This means that laws from any time period may need to be consulted to give a full picture of the current law, so there is more to making needed legal data available than starting a website and publishing the laws as they are passed on a go forward basis. Instead, there is a great deal of investment involved in just obtaining the law, and even in jurisdictions that have been investing in making

DOI: 10.4324/9781003127307-8

Figure 8.1 View of the Capital Building in Washington, DC. Photographer Chris Grafton, Unsplash

it available for years there are often still significant gaps that are only now being filled.

8.2 The nature of data based applications

Data based applications have drawn criticism for reasons such as bias against particular groups and the way they are frequently closed to scrutiny because of intellectual property interests on the part of the companies that develop them. It is important to remember that this situation is often due to political and social constraints. It is not necessarily a limitation of the technology itself, and different methodologies can support more or less transparency about how decisions are made. The issue that is almost inescapable is that machine learning techniques in particular often use criteria for decision making that we think inappropriate or irrelevant:

> The models created by machine learning are not mysterious black boxes. It is quite possible to crack them open and ask how they work. But they work so well because they are under no obligation to condense the world into a crisp definition. A model of a complex, over determined concept is likely to be just as over determined itself.
>
> (Underwood 2019, 49)

The adoption of tools that cannot be adequately examined for high stakes applications, especially those used by states, will need to be thoroughly examined for fairness if they are to be sustainable solutions. A possible solution is to only use open source software and solutions for these applications to allow for scrutiny of the criteria used and outcomes. It will be interesting to see how this will move forward. It will be important not only for political and social concerns, but also for the validity of findings: "Because the relationships relied upon in Big Data are entirely empirical and both concurrent and predictive validity are time dependent. . . there is no reason the correlations that underlie Big Data solutions should persist beyond the sample period." (Crews 2018, 94)

8.3 Access to data

Even where the law is available in electronic formats, it is frequently not accessible for use in application development and research to the degree that those looking to use it may wish it to be. Many countries' legal publishing traditions started from a background of private publishers making volumes available for sale when governments did not. In common law countries, the most frequent model for the start of publishing case law was for private interests to start publishing the law because governments had no interest in doing it.

Issues like this have continued to the present day in many parts of the world, with concerns like disagreements about the intellectual property status of primary law and limits on access to documents being ongoing in many jurisdictions. This leads to situations like the litigation in *Georgia v. Public.Resource. Org, Inc.* where Carl Malamud was accused of terrorism for publishing the *Code* of the American state of Georgia in 2019 after the state had entered into an agreement with a private publisher to publish the state *Code* and provide annotations. The *Code* itself was not protected by copyright, but the annotations were (Liptak 2019). The Supreme Court of the United States found in Malamud's favor in that case (Georgia et al. v. Public.Resource.Org, Inc. 2020).

This complexity leads to private and corporate interests in public data that will be difficult to extricate, illustrating the tension between corporate investment and profits and public spending and interests that have been ongoing in many parts of the world. There does not seem to be a great push among governments and courts outside a few jurisdictions, such as the United States, the European Union, Singapore, and recently the United Kingdom, to make law widely available for private use as data sources, which would allow easier access for exploration of new uses for the data.

In many countries the main publishers of primary law continue to be outside government, with non-profit organizations such as CanLII in Canada, AustLII in Australia, and BAILII in the United Kingdom, and a combination of private publishers and non-profit organizations filling that role in the United States. The fact that in many cases the issuing governments have not made the law available for wider development, and, in fact, may not have preserved copies of the documents in a way that would allow for further distribution means that these organizations have faced pressures to redistribute the law without further support or adequate policy guidance from governments on issues such as privacy.

This has led to an environment where organizations that have digital copies of primary law have had conflict with those who do not and who are not willing or able to build the necessary relationships with issuing bodies and invest in building their own collections. Some have grown impatient with the status quo and have sought to build collections of law in other ways. This has led to tension between those who cannot get the content without developing relationships with issuing bodies, scanning books and processing the scans, or scraping content from websites against their terms of service.

8.4 Privacy

> Cory Doctorow has written about how data should not be considered as a resource so much as toxic waste for the aggregators who must manage adequately discarding it (Doctorow 2020).

Privacy laws significantly affect what legal data is available for analysis, particularly for case law. In common law countries court proceedings have generally been accessible to the public in the absence of compelling reasons to the contrary. However, as more case law is available, privacy concerns about having this information online have been raised. How this is treated varies by jurisdiction, with the United States having quite open access, and many countries in the European Union such as Austria removing all identifying information from cases before they are published.

This is important because most legal documents are public, and many of them contain significant sensitive personal information. Without adequate leadership from governments on how legal documents should be handled, this personal information is an ongoing risk to be managed, and that risk places limits on their reuse as data. In environments where privacy rights and open publishing of legal documents are in tension, this will continue to limit legal technology innovation.

One approach to lessen privacy concerns associated with court data in particular is redaction of identifying information. Countries use different criteria to decide when to redact documents:

- In Austria identifying data is removed from court decisions before it is published by the government even for institutional entities
- In Australia the courts redact their own decisions before publication, which means that there is consistently one good copy available (Mobray and Chung 2021)
- In South Africa publishers redact identifying information where appropriate as courts do not have capacity to do it themselves (Mobray and Chung 2021)

- In Uganda judges have been resistant to any changes to their judgments as issued, and they refuse to allow identifying information to be removed even in cases of decisions concerning minors, rapes, and adoptions (Badeva-Bright 2021)

Automated redaction of identifying information in court decisions is an important area of ongoing study, which may alleviate some of these concerns.

Michael Lissner, the executive director at the Free Law Project in the United States, finds that the current environment for privacy associated with court data in that country is problematic. For example, documents in a bankruptcy case might be filed with identifying information like social security numbers included, which should be under sealing orders. But it can take years for the documents to show up on the government sites so these issues can be missed, but if the documents were published immediately these issues would be caught and resolved. He observed that many lawyers filing documents feel like it is a closed system (Lissner 2021).

Governments and courts that have not done so already will need to resolve the issues around privacy in primary law before it can be widely and effectively used in data driven applications. It is to be hoped that this will happen soon, as this is one of the more promising potential sources of increased efficiency in law, which has the potential to increase access for the many people around the world who are currently underserved. There are some promising technical means of address these needs, but without address privacy issues there will likely continue to be limits on access to many sources of data that could be used to do research into creating the data fed tools that could fulfill this promise.

8.5 Jurisdiction

There is a great deal of variety among jurisdictions in how provision of access to primary legal data has been managed. This is due to many local conditions beyond the legal status of primary law. Here are some of the other considerations that affect the availability of law for analysis.

Infrastructure

Levels of investment in technological infrastructure vary greatly, as does the amount of effort that has been put into digitizing historical laws and making them available in a format suitable for analysis. In many countries, much of the historical, and even some of the current, legal literature continues to be available only in print or in scanned image PDFs which are not machine readable. This paired with the possibility that legal or licensing restrictions may limit how legal materials can be used for analysis, means that the number of jurisdictions where the law is readily available for use is quite small. It is not possible to give a full accounting of the local situations in a single volume, and they change regularly, so it will be necessary to do research into local avail-ability and access before committing to a project.

Another important element of infrastructure in primary law is legal publish-ing, especially of primary law. When looking at statistical elements of the jus-tice system, many queries are not easy to answer from published legal literature: not all court decisions are published or available, especially in routine matters in lower levels of court. And this kind of data which would be particularly interesting to social scientists is often not recorded for analysis (Sutherland 2018).

Beyond primary law, there are many other possible sources of data about the legal system that may or may not be available. In some jurisdictions that have made more investment in open data, some statistical information about topics like court processes and the criminal system is starting to be available. How-ever, in many places this is still not the case, and this does not mean that all the data to answer a particular question will be available.

Legacy systems

As organizations around the world have been using computers for longer, they build legacies of investment and deficits in information technology sys-tems in governments, courts, and businesses that create opportunities and liabilities. It can be difficult or impossible to extract data from these systems adequately to enable them to be rebuilt, so there are regular job postings looking for developers who can work in legacy coding languages to maintain them.

This is not just an issue for governments — businesses like law firms and publishers also create these dynamics and may not be able to migrate their data easily. Decisions made decades ago continue to affect organizations in the pre-sent. For example, legal publishing has substantial legacy documents in print that may or may not be available electronically, and in many cases when they are published electronically, they are published as PDF files or in proprietary systems. These choices limit the usefulness and availability of these documents as source data. In many cases, these are the result of business decisions that were made with the goal of protecting investment in their creation. There are also many instances where these decisions reflect the views of what the content is likely to be used for or particular technological visions of what will make systems most useful.

Law firms have extensive document management systems, which have com-plex interrelationships among documents and business processes like client management. Law firms' business processes can vary widely, because they also have significant differences in what data they have about their operations. This can depend on the value they have placed on it and what systems they use. This data is also proprietary and is generally not available for outside researchers.

These differences appear among law firms in the same places, but they are also affected by culture and local conditions.

Government controls

Governments in different jurisdictions use different mechanisms to control the use of primary law, and each jurisdiction has different systems in place affecting how accessible legal data is. These constraints are further complicated through license agreements that data suppliers may use to limit some uses of the information they make available. These restrictions can be motivated by concerns such as privacy, maintaining certain public perceptions of the courts, and protecting commercial interests.

Privacy is a common concern driving controls on availability of legal data internationally. For example, in 2015 the Privacy Commissioner of Canada found that in Canada there is a right to privacy in the contents of court judgments where they had been published online without limits to searching on the open web (Complaints against Globe24h.com 2015).

In addition to privacy protections, the European Union the GDPR gives data subjects wide ranging rights on how their data is used, and this includes potential applications for legal data:

> The data subject should have the right not to be subject to a decision, which may include a measure, evaluating personal aspects relating to him or her which is based solely on automated processing and which produces legal effects concerning him or her or similarly significantly affects him or her
>
> (General Data Protection Regulation 2016, s. 71).

Looking forward, at the time of writing the European Union has published proposed harmonized regulations for artificial intelligence across the region, and they include the following applications applicable to the legal sector as requiring particular regulation:

- Law enforcement
- Migration, asylum and border control management
- Administration of justice and democratic processes (European Commission 2021)

Many developers are particularly eager to leverage machine learning techniques, but if machine learning is going to be widely used in law, thought will have to be put into how data is made available and how it is used. As the originators of this data, government bodies, such as parliaments, courts, and tribunals, need to take the lead in making sure it is available in a way that works for communities. There are important discussions to have on how knowledgeable people need to be about the tools they use, how transparent suppliers need to be about what data and programs they have used in development, and how much users can reply on the tools created with these systems. Regulation is one way to limit access to artificial intelligence entrants, while allowing lawyers to still use machine inputs to make their work more cost effective (McGinnis and Pearce 2019, 3042).

8.6 Primary law

In England and Wales the publication of case law started with court reporters recording and publishing court cases with origins that date back to Edward II (1307–1325). This was the model for the development of case law publishing in common law countries. Court reporters sat in courtrooms and recorded what they heard then made the judgements available for sale. Commercial publication was also the model for the development of the publication of parliamentary debates in Britain. Publication of which before late 18th Century was a was punishable by both houses of Parliament as a breach of parliamentary privilege (Wikipedia 2020).

This legacy should not be forgotten in looking at how to use the law as data now, because there is no set point at which the law stops being relevant. If it is not changed or overturned, it continues to be in force into the present. The work of developing electronic collections of law to the point where available data is sufficient to support uses like legal research without regular access to extensive print collections, and by extension sufficient for sophisticated applications based on the current law, has taken decades in most jurisdictions, and is in many cases still not complete. It continues to be common for people researching complex issues to have to refer to print volumes for historical law, and the investment required to add still more material gets higher for content that is less accessed. In many jurisdictions, having sufficient primary law coverage for sophisticated uses is years away, even where there is political will to make it happen.

This is important because many of the discussions about the future of law and legal practice driven by technological developments depend on the availability of data to support them. As time passes, laws may be published in more data compliant standards, but access to and understanding of existing legacy data in plain text formats will continue to be necessary far into the future. There is speculation that technology will solve problems associated with the legal system, but it will not be built without the data to support it. This goes beyond simply publishing court judgments online in machine readable formats. There are real concerns about the potential artificial intelligence applications that may be built using the data and that technology alone will not solve issues associated with artificial intelligence systems and trustworthiness. Governance and regulation are also needed (Chatila 2020).

Court decisions are some of the most targeted sources for data analysis in law. That said, they are not always easy to access for this purpose. In some cases there are downloads of relatively full datasets that are available, while in others they may be in a database, which may need to have the data exported or extracted in other ways. It is important to consult the terms of service or other restrictions on the use of any sources of this data that you access. Infringing these limits may have legal consequences, but it may also have consequences for a project if researchers are blocked from accessing the data going forward. In some situations, data may not be available without permission from issuing bodies or payments for licensing rights, and in others it may not be available for this use at all.

8.7 Practice data

Data generated by the work of lawyers and staff in practice environments is one of the most obvious sources of data in the legal industry, and one that provides clear potential for organizations like firms and ministries of justice to improve their processes and performance. That said, there are issues associated with its use that limit its reach as a potential source of efficiency gains.

The readiness to integrate business data into legal practice depends on the segment of the market. Global law firms are generally quite sophisticated and ready to do this, and small law firms and solo lawyers know their data and can have an idea of how it could be used, but medium sized law firms tend to have a lot of data, but less ability to leverage it or even know what they have. The cultural change around integrating this data into practice is ongoing, and conversations are now happening where five years ago they were not. One of the big drivers of this change is clients who have sophisticated data use internally and want firms to reflect that too (Hodgins 2021).

Beyond the internal politics around business decisions to use data in certain ways and invest in the technical and data infrastructure to make a program viable, there are also considerable considerations related to client confidentiality that need to be considered. The requirements for this kind of program vary by jurisdiction as law practice is highly regulated and differs by jurisdiction, so any program like this will need to take these considerations into account.

> "if you want to sell such 'big data' to an old school lawyer or law firm, don't sell data. Sell history." (Walker 2019, 242)

8.8 The research landscape

Data driven research in law, whether it is aimed at understanding the law itself or how it affects people and societies, is developing quickly. It is however not evenly distributed: different countries, regions, institutions, and individuals, have very different levels of expertise, resources, and existing research, to build on. While research in this area continues to develop, there is still resistance to data driven research in law from many sources. This is especially true of the use of experimental methodologies. For example, the many people who object to double blind A/B testing do so even where they do not object to any of the possible options. This can lead to universal implementation of untested interventions as a way to avoid negative perceptions of experimental methodologies and higher risks than if experiments had been carried out (Meyer et al. 2019).

This resistance to the use of data in research in society is paired with resistance to the acceptance of developing real world applications as legitimate research topics for artificial intelligence. Many reviewers and researchers believe that real world applications are not relevant for publishing and presenting. They instead focus on novel algorithms and other primary research, using classic and static benchmark datasets that can bake in bias as they are not tested against live data. Practical applications of this technology would help move the field forward as a whole (Kerner 2020).

8.9 Working toward change

> "Sometimes trends are really boring, so we don't pay any attention to them." (Webb 2016, 65)

Cultural expectations of how legal data is treated affect what is available. Until relatively recently, in many parts of the world legal information has primarily been made available through commercial means. The expectation that legal information is valuable and that it is acceptable that people be required to pay for it may continue to limit access. However going forward, there will likely be significant changes to the ways legal data is made available and how access to it is limited. Balancing the needs of data subjects, the needs of the legal system for adequate record keeping, the needs of the legal sector, and the need for innovation to improve access to justice will be difficult, with different jurisdictions choosing to weight these considerations in different ways.

Many developers and researchers want to drive technological change, and they want to be successful in one way or another. In many cases, they are impatient and do not want to wait for the time to be right for governments and courts to address these concerns, and maybe without them pushing the time may never be right. It is then up to governments and professional governing bodies to set limits on these applications in the way they would with another innovation like alternate business models.

There will need to be oversight of these tools, especially if the people using them are not going to develop the expertise to confidently select tools that will work for their needs. This could take many forms, such as government or professional body regulation, or a certification from an issuing body that guarantees that a product meets some criteria for quality.

Though there are criticisms of many existing data based tools and their potential social consequences, there are other possibilities that may have more positive outcomes. Paying attention to technological developments and how policy decisions impact them is crucial. Leaders should not wait to confront the future until they must, as by that point the moment has already passed (Webb 2016, 18).

8.10 Conclusion

Much of the discussion around the law and politics of legal data is related to perceptions of risk. There are two kinds of risks in the practice of law: risks of knowledge and risks of ignorance. Risks associated with ignorance have gone up. Risks of knowledge have stayed the same (Grady 2018, 19). Many issues around legal data come down to people's different motivations. Whether people are more concerned about privacy or getting open access to data depends on what their background is and what they want to achieve. The stakes are high for data based applications in law, and it is not an acceptable solution to break the proverbial eggs and fix things in the future as issues become clear. There are reasons for the rules about things like what evidence is admissable in court and they continue to matter as technological changes comes.

> "When it comes to killing cancer cells or predicting the weather... we do not need to understand the exact mechanism of an AI in order to empower it to solve our problems. But when it comes to important decisions about people, the inexplicable is inappropriate." (Pasquale 2020, 18)

Works cited

Badeva-Bright, Mariya. 2021. (Co-founder Laws.Africa and Project Director AfricanLII, University of Cape Town), in discussion with the author.

Chatila, Raja. 2020. "Can AI Systems Be Trustworthy?" Presented at the JURIX 2020: 33rd International Conference on Legal Knowledge and Information Systems, Virtual, December 11.

Complaints against Globe24h.com. 2015. CanLII 33260 (PCC). Privacy Commissioner of Canada.

Crews, Aaron. 2018. "The Big Move Toward Big Data in Employment." In *Data-Driven Law: Data Analytics and the New Legal Services*, edited by Edward Walters, 59–102. Boca Raton, FL: Auerbach Publications.

European Commission. 2021. "Annexes to the Proposal for a Regulation of the European Parliament and of the Council Laying Down Harmonised Rules on Artificial Intelligence (Artificial Intelligence Act) and Amending Certain Union Legislative Acts." COM(2021) 206 final. Brussels: European Commission.

General Data Protection Regulation, Regulation (EU) 2016/679 of the European Parliament and of the Council of 27 April 2016 on the Protection of Natural Persons with Regard to the Processing of Personal Data and on the Free Movement of Such Data, and Repealing Directive 95/46/EC. 2016. EUR-Lex - 02016R0679–20160504. http://data.europa.eu/eli/reg/2016/679/oj.

Georgia et al. v. Public.Resource.Org, Inc. 2020. Supreme Court of the United States.

Grady, Kenneth A. 2018. "Mining Legal Data: Collecting and Analyzing 21st Century Gold." In *Data-Driven Law: Data Analytics and the New Legal Services*, edited by Edward Walters, 11–32. Boca Raton, FL: Auerbach Publications.

"Hansard." 2020. In Wikipedia. Wikipedia Foundation. https://en.wikipedia.org/w/index.php?title=Hansard&oldid=991040030.

Hodgins, Kristin. 2021. *Director of Legal Operations*, Government of British Columbia, Canada, in discussion with the author.

Kerner, Hannah. 2020. "Too Many AI Researchers Think Real-World Problems Are Not Relevant." *MIT Technology Review*, August 18, 2020. https://www.technologyreview.com/2020/08/18/1007196/ai-research-machine-learning-applications-problems-opinion/.

Lefrak, Mikaela. 2021. "D.C. Bills In Limbo As Fences Block Hand-Delivery To Congress." *DCist* (blog). February 1, 2021. https://dcist.com/story/21/02/01/dc-laws-in-limbo-no-delivery-to-congress/.

Liptak, Adam. 2019. "Accused of 'Terrorism' for Putting Legal Materials Online (Published 2019)." *The New York Times*, May 13, 2019, sec. U.S. https://www.nytimes.com/2019/05/13/us/politics/georgia-official-code-copyright.html.

Lissner, Michael. 2021. (Executive Director at Free Law Project), in discussion with the author.

McGinnis, John O., and Russell G. Pearce. 2019. "The Great Disruption: How Machine Intelligence Will Transform the Role of Lawyers in the Delivery of Legal Services." *Actual Problems of Economics and Law* 13 (2). https://doi.org/10.21202/1993-047X.13.2019.2.1230-1250.

Meyer, Michelle N., Patrick R. Heck, Geoffrey S. Holtzman, Stephen M. Anderson, William Cai, Duncan J. Watts, and Christopher F. Chabris. 2019. "Objecting to Experiments That Compare Two Unobjectionable Policies or Treatments." *Proceedings of the National Academy of Sciences* 116 (22): 10723–10728. https://doi.org/10.1073/pnas.1820701116.

Mobray, Andrew, and Philip Chung. 2021. (Co-Director and Executive Director AustLII [Australasian Legal Information Institute]), in discussion with the author.

Sutherland, Sarah. 2018. "So There's Been Some Buzz about Legal Data Lately …." *Slaw* (blog). March 29, 2018. http://www.slaw.ca/2018/03/29/so-theres-been-some-buzz-about-legal-data-lately/.

Underwood, Ted. 2019. *Distant Horizons: Digital Evidence and Literary Change*. Chicago: University of Chicago Press. https://www.amazon.ca/Distant-Horizons-Digital-Evidence-Literary/dp/022661283X/ref=tmm_pap_swatch_0?_encoding=UTF8&qid=&sr=.

Webb, Amy. 2016. *The Signals Are Talking: Why Today's Fringe Is Tomorrow's Mainstream*. New York: PublicAffairs.

Chapter 9

Vision for the future

9.1 Introduction

I would argue that change is not accelerating with the adoption of the technologies discussed in this book, though it may feel that way. The changes that are happening now with ongoing developments in computing have been developing for at least 70 years, since the first explorations of artificial intelligence in the 1950s. The work that has been getting more attention recently of looking at how to encode semantic content in the law is a continuation of work that started in the 1980s (Morris 2021).

In *The Rise and Fall of American Growth*, Robert J. Gordon argues that compared to the changes that happened in the early 20th Century with the introduction of innovations like widespread access to electricity and running water, the changes that we are experiencing are minor. Consider that housewives or, usually female, servants had to manually carry all clean water used for cooking, washing, and cleaning, into dwellings each day, then they had to carry out all the waste water as well (Gordon 2016). We are unlikely to face anything this transformative arising from artificial intelligence and computing.

The change that does appear to be accelerating is that developments in computing are starting to affect the jobs and business models of lawyers directly, where they have already made a difference for many of the people who work with them like assistants and librarians. Many lawyers have done well by following their existing business models, and they may not be able to follow those paths anymore.

There is currently much discussion of how the law, legal practice, and governance, will be transformed in the future, but less about how the underlying infrastructure of data that will be required to support it and make it fair will be developed. With some exceptions, governments internationally show little evidence of wanting to invest in providing this infrastructure, and, even if it is made available in some places, it will be uneven across jurisdictions far into the future. That said, the law has lagged behind other areas of research and industry in the adoption of data based research and decision making, but this trend does not have to continue, and there are increasing pressures to make sure it does not. There are many opportunities to use data to improve businesses and

DOI: 10.4324/9781003127307-9

understand the environment through research now, and there will be more in the future as some of the technical limitations are addressed.

9.2 Thinking about the future

Before I give my predictions about the future I want to talk a bit about the thought processes and sources I used in writing this chapter. When thinking about the future, I find it useful to think of what outcomes are probable. The probable future is what is likely to happen if current trends continue. There are also improbable futures that could, but probably will not happen, but there is an infinite number of events and an infinite number of points in time, which mean that unlikely events will happen regularly.

The paired forces of inertia and randomness mean that while the future is likely to follow long term trends, with an overarching pressure to deviate toward historical means. This is paired with the influence of improbable events happening at frequent, if random, intervals, which may have a disproportionate influence on outcomes. The impact of unforeseen highly improbable events was discussed influentially by Nassim Nicholas Taleb in his book *The Black Swan* (Taleb 2010).

It makes good news stories to forecast recent trends into the future to an unreasonable degree. I think of this as thinking that the future will be more like the present than the present is. This is not a reasonable way to approach our understanding of what will happen over time. In many cases these trends have already reached their maximum extent when these articles are written.

These deviations from long term trends tend to revert to what would be expected based on long term forces, because things like culture, the environment, and technological developments are powerful influences on events and relatively constant, and they tend to override short term changes. Partly this is because of how small changes over time compound to have significant effects. Culture also tends to be conservative, and individual events tend to have less impact than we think they will.

So my perspective on the future combines the force of long term historical trends, the likelihood that the trends that seem most interesting to us are anomalies that will soon exhaust themselves, consistency in human nature paired with long-term changes in culture, and the force of the unexpected to shift things in ways we do not anticipate. These forces do not combine to make the best clickbait forecasting stories, but they do make a framework that allows me to think about the future in a structured way.

As Bill Gates wrote in *The Road Ahead*: "We always overestimate the change that will occur in the next two years and underestimate the change that will occur in the next ten." (Gates 1995)

9.3 Forecasting

There are three types of forecasts:

- Probable futures, which are near term and involve current trends that are likely to continue
- Plausible futures, for which we have an understanding of the forces involved and the mechanics of how they would happen
- Possible futures, which may not happen in our lifetimes and are based on emerging technologies and cultural changes that could happen (Webb 2019, 84–5)

Both predicting the future and the development of the future itself requires human insight and imagination. Many believe that computer algorithms have the power to take over these functions, but:

> Simply put, an algorithm is a set of rules that define a sequence of operations that have to be followed in a particular order. Combined with machine learning, artificial intelligence, and extremely powerful computers, algorithms can sort through massive, sprawling datasets to answer a number of complicated questions.
>
> (Webb 2016, 86)

Essentially, algorithms make recommendations and derive insights based on existing data, which, as has been discussed elsewhere in this book, is limited to the kinds of things that generate data and by quality concerns, even where it can be collected.

9.4 Technology adoption dynamics

The future of technology in law lies in two main dynamics. The first is the pattern that technology follows as it develops and is adopted in other disciplines, and then is transferred into legal applications. The second dynamic is the legal and social patterns that dictate what applications are accepted by law makers, the legal community, and society. One of the most useful ways to consider the future of technological development is to consider what primary research is being completed now. There is extensive research that is not being widely adopted than remains to be deployed in the future (Soh 2021).

See Table 9.1 for a breakdown of possible futures.

To some degree the future of legal technology can be seen by looking at what is being and has been published and patented in computer science over the last several years. This can then be paired with the understanding that law is a highly regulated field with powerful human actors who have entrenched ideas about how things should be handled. In most technology driven fields, such as biotechnology, the

Table 9.1 Possible futures for legal technology.

	Low technology adoption	High technology adoption
High cultural acceptance	Focus on design and social change in justice design Frustration for justice participants Lack of productivity gains	Increases in productivity in legal space Potential underinvestment in experience design Potential widening divide between people who can access legal services and those who cannot Potential for divergence in access as tools are not available to everyone
Low cultural acceptance	Maintenance of status quo Reliance on design and social elements of change Low efficiency gains Productivity in other parts of the economy not reflected in law, so increases the proportion of the economy the legal system comprises (Baumol et al. 2013)	Regulation of legal technology to stop what is not culturally accepted Reduced trust in justice being carried out Justice participants who cannot or will not accept technology being left behind

patterns of technology adoption usually follow a defined curve with different centers of research taking different roles:

- University researchers carry out primary research exploring new fields
- Then government research labs carry the research forward toward practical applicability
- Government technology is then transferred to start ups that develop it further
- After the technology is past proof of concept stage, the startups either commercialize it themselves or sell the companies or technology to larger companies that take it to market

This process often takes as long as 20 years.

The problem in law is that there have been relatively few academic researchers interested in exploring technology innovation. Instead, their focus has usually been on exploring the ways the laws themselves behave and can be innovated. There have also been few centers of innovation and research into legal innovation within governments to explore developing technology in this sector. Instead, governmental agencies working in law tend to focus on applying or developing the law itself.

This has left startups and established companies as some of the primary drivers of legal technology, which has led to an unbalanced innovation space where commercial interests have taken the lead and where there has been less discussion of how innovation can best serve communities. The major exception to this is the innovative tools being developed in the legal non-profit and legal aid spaces. The pressures of limited resources and essentially unlimited need have pushed the development of technology tools that can extend their reach and free time for complicated issues.

As we think about the kinds of changes that improved collection of, access to, and use of legal data generate, there is inevitably discussion of reduced need for people to do certain types of tasks and the economic repercussions of these changes. Different kinds of technologies have different effects:

> The extent to which labor-saving technologies will cause dislocation depends on whether they are enabling or replacing. Replacing technologies render jobs and skills redundant. Enabling technologies, in contrast, make people more productive in existing tasks or create entirely new jobs for them.
>
> (Frey 2019, 13)

Developing the understanding of potential for new technologies and their adoption in disciplines is frequently slow. Technologies that are encapsulated within themselves that can be implemented without behavior change, like flat screen monitors, are easy to roll out and can be widely and quickly adopted. Technology changes that require extensive training and development of new knowledge, like the integration of statistical methods into peoples' work, are more difficult and take considerably longer (Underwood 2019, 144–45).

9.5 Issues

There are many issues facing the development of the law and the legal system. Here are some that are likely to have significant impacts on this field into the future.

Data availability

Unless there are significant changes in the legal innovation process, there are unlikely to be substantial primary technology developments that come from the legal space rather than the refinement of existing tools developed in other disciplines and industries. Partly this is because the law is too complicated to be useful as an initial dataset for development of new computing techniques where the use of the tool in law is not a requirement for its development. This is before considering that there are problems with accessing legal data, particularly primary law, which are likely to continue into the future.

In addition to the question of whether existing laws are available for use as data, there are questions about how suitable the existing bodies of documents and other formats are. From case law to internal documents, the ways documents and systems have been designed limits their re-use as data. To address this, many people are pushing governments to provide laws in more data-centric formats. At its simplest level, this includes publishing legal documents in XML tagged versions that can be more easily integrated into applications. These are relatively simple improvements, but they still have the potential to improve access and accessibility significantly.

There are also calls for making laws in the form of code in order to make it more intelligible and useful as data, which has not been widely implemented beyond proofs of concept. As these kinds of initiatives progress more will be possible. To a large degree, the primary consideration for how the law is published has not been to make it accessible. Rather it has been designed as a record that good governance is done. Changing this priority will have long lasting repercussions that cannot be ignored if we care about accountability in governments and courts.

Going forward there will be drivers of data availability that will lead to it being available or not. These include the following.

Privacy laws

Privacy laws significantly impact how much law is available and the detail of what is included when it is published. There are significant risks for data driven initiatives if privacy laws are in conflict with a given use. Any project in this space should consider existing privacy laws and probable future privacy developments before extensive investment is made. Many countries will review their privacy laws in the near to medium terms, and it is likely they will become more restrictive in many places. This will place considerable limits on how the integration of evidence based understanding can be integrated into legal scholarship and practice.

Many countries adhere to the "Open Court Principle," but it was developed in a time with greater obscurity than is the case now. Over time, more granular publication of legal data with improved systems like ontologies could make the law more accessible, usable, and computationally tractable, but it will also make it more visible. Law makers will have to reconcile these needs because existing rules were created when the potential harms of individuals broadcasting to millions of people were not possible (Morris 2021).

Available investment

In recent years there has been significant investment in some parts of the legal data space, notable examples include technology startups in North America and the publication of primary law by European governments. Outside of these areas there has been significantly less investment. Whether funds are available for meaningful development or not will significantly affect outcomes.

Cultural acceptance

There will need to be cultural acceptance of the use of data in law on the part of the legal community and wider societies if the promise of legal data is going to be realized. Successful integration will require prioritizing the creation and dissemination of data in formats that are usable and reliable. It will also involve acceptance of data based recommendations as a basis for decision making, while understanding the limits of this approach. Not everyone needs to accept the use of data in this way, but enough will need to, or there will be insufficient movement to drive real change.

Competing priorities

There are many possible priorities for development in the legal system, and these priorities will drive what is available. There is a great deal that can be done with well-designed systems and current technology that can be implemented more quickly that advanced data driven applications. It may be that these are expedited for delivery with the limited resources organizations such as governments are willing to devote to these initiatives.

Regulation of technology

There are many criteria that can be used when deciding how regulation of legal technology and publication and use of legal data should be handled. One big source of divergence will be between a future where legal technology is regulated with the goal of maximizing profits and a future where it is regulated with the goal of maximizing social utility. These priorities are not mutually exclusive: there are potential futures where the legal sector is both profitable and good for society, and where the legal sector is both unprofitable and bad for society.

There can also be distinctions between maximizing social utility for existing actors in the legal system and developing a future in ways designed to help wider communities. These tensions have played out in other times with other technological developments. One reason the Industrial Revolution started in England instead of somewhere else is because the English government started catering to the interests of industrialists who wanted to mechanize instead of the interests of the workers who would be displaced (Frey 2019, 10).

Many people who call for the development of legal technology and access to legal data seem to believe that technology always serves the same purposes and generates the same outcomes. But in contrast to the model endorsed by contemporary capitalism, in classical times technological advances typically served the public rather than to develop productivity. Technology was used by leaders to safeguard political power (Frey 2019, 37). Dynamics like this, driven by cultural expectations, will drive regulatory changes which will be especially important as law is such a strongly regulated sector.

Social concerns

There are important social concerns about the use of data based applications in law. Using data to drive better understanding and decision making in law opens opportunities, but there are legitimate concerns. The most successful and least problematic data applications in law so far are used by relatively sophisticated users to enhance decision making, understanding, and research. There are more problems when the primary users of applications are people who have little choice or recourse when things go wrong. Legal systems should serve the needs of the people who are affected by them, and these tensions will need to be addressed if data is to be used to dramatically change systems.

9.6 Divergence

There are, and will continue to be, significant differences in access and the possibilities that legal data enable based on many factors. Some of the main sources of divergence are discussed below.

Jurisdiction

One of the biggest drivers of divergence going forward in this space is jurisdiction. There are significant differences between access and publishing of data and technological implementation around the world, but it does not have to be that way. In the first half of the 20th century in contrast, much of the world was part of European empires which dictated how legal systems would be, and most of these places had similar print distribution models. This meant that there was less difference between regions' legal systems and the availability of their laws. At that time it was relatively common for Canadian courts to cite Indian case law for example. After decades of regional divergence this is no longer the case, though there continue to be exceptions: Singapore is notable for heavy reliance on international law in their courts (Soh 2021).

The different levels of access to technology among countries creates barriers to equitable access to technological infrastructure that significantly affect the future of technology development in law. Beyond this divergence in legal systems which necessitates additional development in each jurisdiction, there will also continue to be divergence in technology investment and adoption. Consider the difference in capacity between the technological centers in California and New York and rural parts of the United States, then consider that the differences between the technological centers in Bangalore or Delhi and rural and remote India are significantly greater.

Around the world are also frequently preferences for local legal developments reflecting national and regional priorities paired with strong advantages to consistent rules across borders. There are also often preferences for custom made technology solutions designed for specific legal systems and languages, and different levels of resources allocated to technology implementation and levels of cultural acceptance of technology. So it is probable that the differences between places will continue to increase and that the future of legal data and technology is increased divergence based on where you are.

That said, there is no reason that current patterns of technology use and investment will have to continue. There is a real possibility that countries that have lagged in adoption of technology until now will be able to pass places that have more existing infrastructure, if they can adopt the best technology without having to accommodate and maintain extensive legacy systems.

Population segments

Different groups of people will be affected by any changes in different ways, and each will have different influences on potential outcomes. The first of the two main groups affected are internal to the justice system: the legal profession courts, and legislative bodies. The second is external, though participating, in it: current clients, potential clients, companies, and the public at large.

The legal profession, courts, and legislative bodies set the priorities of the current system in many ways. It is their education, training, professional expectations, priorities, and experience, that build and maintain the justice system. There are many observations that this group is more conservative than is appropriate given the pace of technological change, but there are also good reasons why societies that have been developing over hundreds of years would want to maintain a link with their pasts. Many of the people who make those observations are unfamiliar with the legal system and the reasons why certain systems exist. One important distinction is that traditionally the priority for primary law publication has not been to communicate the law, instead it served to communicate that appropriate process has been followed. Unless the requirement to document good process are met by a new system, it is unlikely to ever be widely accepted and adopted.

The other main group affected by this discussion is the public. The public can be further divided into active or prospective justice system participants and non-participants. Participants can then be further divided into current and potential clients of lawyers or other service providers, and people who do not get professional help. Members of the public who are not currently involved in the legal system still need information about the laws that govern them and assistance in making decisions with legal consideration. There is a great deal of room for improvement in how legal systems interact with people, and it is to be hoped that the innovations considered in this book and others that have not been contemplated yet will allow this to happen.

A discussion of groups of people affected by these changes would not be complete in a book like this without discussing the likely outcomes for groups involved in distributing and providing access to legal information, including libraries and publishers. These groups are unlikely to be able to significantly drive outcomes in how data is created, used, and influence legal processes, but there are real possibilities to benefit from the changes for those who can leap at the right time.

Legal system

The next driver is related to jurisdiction: different legal systems have significant effects on how data use is implemented in different jurisdictions. Whether a legal system is common law or civil law and whether it is converging or diverging with other systems affects how legal data is published and used. Part of the complexity surrounding these issues is because the law is dynamic and changes frequently. It is an ongoing problem faced by legal publishers to ensure that the versions of the laws on their websites are current. The task of maintaining currency will be significantly more challenging for advanced applications that need to be recalibrated and tested as new laws are passed. Successful legal data systems will need to handle the law's systemic requirements.

In some ways civil law systems seem like they would be better able to manage the complexities of publishing and making use of data, as the amendments would tend to be more planned. Whereas in a common law system there are more sources of law that may be changing at any time in complex and interacting ways. That said, there is evidence that instead of common law becoming more like civil law, the structure of case law in civil law jurisdictions is coming to more closely resemble common law (Beauchamp-Tremblay and Dusséaux 2019). Given that a great deal of legal data is procedural, the suitability of processes for data creation is important for the likelihood of success of any data system.

Culture

Culture is another source of divergence in legal technology and data systems. Different countries, regions, and professions have divergent cultures that affect likely outcomes for legal technology and data systems. Understanding and respecting these cultures are some of the most important things to do to achieve successful implementation. Change is often resisted, especially by people who are invested in the status quo, but the attitudes and approaches of the people initiating change are also important.

One of the most harmful things that has happened culturally regarding moving the data driven agenda forward in law is an overly confrontational attitude. Positioning one's self as a "burn the ships" type of person "induces social hostility from the very people who can prevent you from succeeding" (Walker 2019, 37).

9.7 Predictions

Predictions run over different time periods, so I have divided mine in the same way. It is difficult to forecast, especially in the common law, because there are many fault lines that will affect any future state that have not been studied well, such as privacy, rule of law, and judicial independence (Hoadley 2021). That said here are some changes that I anticipate happening in coming years.

Near term

Changing productivity paired with changing market size

In the near term there will be changes in productivity in the legal sector and changing market size. I think the legal market will increase in size while simultaneously increasing in productivity. When considering innovations in legal practice leading to increased automation, it should not be overlooked that there are substantial unmet needs for legal services in society. The market could grow considerably at the same time as it is becoming more productive. However, it is still important to consider that a growing market size may not be sufficient to ensure that the current providers of legal services will not be displaced as new opportunities are being created.

This is not the only possible outcome: the market size could also shrink and there could be no productivity gains. This leads to four possible future states, as you can see in Table 9.2.

As these new opportunities are created, it is not clear where the required expertise in these future states that require extensive expertise in data use will come from:

> the problem is not lack of resources, but is lack of skills. A company that has data but no one to analyze it is in a poor position to take advantage of

Table 9.2 Potential futures for the legal industry.

	Low productivity	*High productivity*
Increasing market size	Increase in proportion of economy directed to legal services Increase of legal workforce	Proportion of economy directed at legal services stays the same Legal workforce stays the same or grows
Decreasing market size	Proportion of economy directed to legal services stays the same or decreases Legal workforce stays the same or shrinks	Proportion of economy directed at legal services decreases Shrinking of legal workforce

that data. If there is no existing expertise internally, it is hard to make intelligent choices about what skills are needed and how to find and hire people with those skills. Hiring good people has always been a critical issue for competitive advantage. But since the widespread availability of data is comparatively recent, this problem is particularly acute.

(Varian 2018, 17)

It will not be possible to automate the entire practice of law, and given that the laws affect us in complex ways I am not sure it is something to aspire to do. That said, it is certainly within reach to significantly improve some problems like bad contract clauses, stupid disputes, and drafting errors (Walker 2019).

For a job to be made redundant, generally 100% of the tasks completed do not have to be taken away. Approximately 40% of the work associated with a job is created by the job itself, so if approximately 60% of the work can be taken away the job can generally be discontinued. Though different organizations use different numbers, the principle is widely followed. A study published in 2015 found that approximately 13% of the tasks lawyers spend their time doing are in danger of being automated (Remus and Levy 2016). How this dynamic will affect individual employees and organizations remains to be seen.

Medium term

Born digital legal data

It seems like an obvious prediction that legal documents and systems will start to be developed with the intention of having them be successfully used as data, but it is not clear how it will be achieved given the apparent lack of motivation for law makers in both legislative bodies and courts to change their processes at a deep enough level to achieve this. That said there are significant potential gains, and it is unlikely that it will not be implemented anywhere.

Publication of law as code promises excellent functionality to use the law for end users, but the publication of the law is designed to show procedural process and how it can be traced. A standalone XML file does not do that. We will have to decide how much we want data driving our systems of governance. Data can drive decisions, but creating good data will require changes to processes, because current data reflects existing processes, and it is not sufficient for this use. Going forward, processes will have to reflect desired outcomes. This will require acceptance and cooperation of many stakeholders, including those who may not be currently considered such as court staff and the civil servants who draft legislation.

Semantic data may be able to integrate artificially generated models of outcomes of legislative interventions as a way to pursue the counterfactuals that have been so missing from assessment of law. These developments will have the potential to free rule makers from some constraints that affect laws as they are developed now. It may also allow for increased certainty on how a particular set of rules will behave once it is in effect. These developments could change the realm of what is possible. Maybe instead of simply making the law more efficient, it could make different kinds of rules possible: if tax codes for example are freed from the necessity of being navigable by human readers, it may be possible for them to become more complex to address more sophisticated policy objectives (Morris 2021).

Long term

The next generation of artificial intelligence

Artificial intelligence is hitting the limit of what can be accomplished with free text analysis, because the programs have no context for what they are analyzing. They have no frame of reference for what things are, instead they only know that the word "apple" is associated with the "pie" and "computer" strings of text. I have heard that the next generation of artificial intelligence will likely require building independent robots so it can explore the world to understand the context for the things it encounters (Sutherland 2018).

Current artificial intelligence systems are looking at a series of binary encoded text and trying to find patterns, but they have no conception of what parts of that text is significant or what any of the words mean. Legal documents are some of the most complex writing in English, and it is unlikely that the nuance of what they mean will be an easy target. One area of research being pursued at the Legal Information Institute at Cornell University is how to develop better ways to tie things in the world to words that are used and defined in the law (Frug 2021).

David Runciman explained these limits with regard to artificial intelligence's approach to understand language this way:

> Alpha-Zero may have overcome thousands of years of human civilisation in a few days, but those same thousands of years of civilisation have taught us to register in an instant forms of communication that no machine is close to being able to comprehend. Chess is a problem to be solved, but language is not and this kind of open-ended intelligence isn't either. Nor is language simply a problem-solving mechanism. It is what enables us to model the world around us; it allows us to decide which problems are the ones worth solving. These are forms of intelligence that machines have yet to master.
>
> (Runciman 2018)

It may be that artificial intelligence may never master those problems of complex thought and language, but it is clear that new techniques for exploring the world through artificial intelligence will be developed, and that eventually it will be deployed in law. Given the relative lack of progress that current artificial intelligence models have made with legal materials, the value of the legal market, and the lack of productivity gains so far, it is likely that attempts will be made to use these new technologies in law relatively soon.

9.8 Conclusion

There is a great deal of talk about how technological developments are inevitable and that law cannot evade them, but many of the people saying these things underestimate the impacts law in turn can and will have on their projects and companies. Many technology companies have found legal loopholes and built their business models around them, but these approaches may not be sustainable depending on how law makers choose to respond. Instead of talking about how technology will affect law, it may be more prescient to ask how law will affect technology.

Law and governance are full of powerful people who may or may not care about data use in law, and they are unlikely to change in ways they do not want to change. Technology developing in a particular direction is not a natural law. Most people looking to the future of the legal industry anticipate there being more use of technology than there is at present, but there is the potential that there will be pushback against the current hype, and artificial intelligence research in particular may neglect promising developments in the future (Walters 2021).

There is a great deal of room for innovation in using data in the legal space, especially if it is considered and we are careful about negative consequences for the individuals and communities affected by it. Innovators are running toward what they see as the future, but there are limits to what data is available to support that work. There will likely always be hard boundaries on the potential for artificial intelligence in law because of the impreciseness of language and thought, and the ambiguity in human relationships. As human beings we lack clarity about what we are looking for and what we want, but we also bring insights that are necessary: "One of the reasons we allow judges to condemn criminals to prison is because a judge can viscerally understand what confinements would feel like" (Pasquale 2020, 216). It will be interesting to see what happens as technological capacity, and, just as importantly, cultural acceptance of it move forward.

Works cited

Baumol, William J., David de Ferranti, MonteMalach, ArielPablos-Méndez, HilaryTabish, and Lilian Gomory Wu. 2013. *The Cost Disease: Why Computers Get Cheaper and Health Care Doesn't*. New Haven London: Yale University Press.

Beauchamp-Tremblay, Xavier, and Antoine Dusséaux. 2019. "Not Your Grandparents' Civil Law: Decisions Are Getting Longer. Why and What Does It Mean in France and Québec?" *Slaw* (blog). June 20, 2019. http://www.slaw.ca/2019/06/20/not-your-grandparents-civil-law-decisions-are-getting-longer-why-and-what-does-it-mean-in-france-and-quebec/.

Frey, Carl Benedikt. 2019. *The Technology Trap: Capital, Labor, and Power in the Age of Automation*. Princeton, NJ: Princeton University Press.

Frug, Sara. 2021. (Co-Director at Legal Information Institute), in conversation with the author.

Gordon, Robert J. 2016. *The Rise and Fall of American Growth: The U.S. Standard of Living since the Civil War*. Princeton: Princeton University Press.

Hoadley, Daniel. 2021. (Head of Litigation Data at Mishcon de Reya LLP), in discussion with the author.

Morris, Jason. 2021. (Principal Research Engineer, Symbolic Artificial Intelligence for the Singapore Management University Centre for Computational Law), in discussion with the author.

Pasquale, Frank. 2020. *New Laws of Robotics: Defending Human Expertise in the Age of AI*. Cambridge, Massachusetts: Belknap Press of Harvard University Press. https://www.amazon.ca/New-Laws-Robotics-Defending-Expertise/dp/0674975227.

Remus, Dana, and Frank S. Levy. 2016. "Can Robots Be Lawyers? Computers, Lawyers, and the Practice of Law." SSRN Scholarly Paper ID 2701092. Rochester, NY: Social Science Research Network. https://doi.org/10.2139/ssrn.2701092.

Runciman, David. 2018. "Diary: AI." *London Review of Books*, January 25, 2018. https://www.lrb.co.uk/the-paper/v40/n02/david-runciman/diary.

Soh, Jerrold. 2021. (Assistant Professor of Law and Deputy Director, Centre for Computational Law at the Singapore Management University), in discussion with the author.

Sutherland, Sarah. 2018. "So There's Been Some Buzz about Legal Data Lately …." *Slaw* (blog). March 29, 2018. http://www.slaw.ca/2018/03/29/so-theres-been-some-buzz-about-legal-data-lately/.

Taleb, Nassim Nicholas. 2010. *The Black Swan: The Impact of the Highly Improbable*. 2nd ed. New York: Random House.

Underwood, Ted. 2019. *Distant Horizons: Digital Evidence and Literary Change*. Chicago: University of Chicago Press. https://www.amazon.ca/Distant-Horizons-Digital-Evidence-Literary/dp/022661283X/ref=tmm_pap_swatch_0?_encoding=UTF8&qid=&sr=.

Varian, Hal. 2018. "Artificial Intelligence, Economics, and Industrial Organization, Working Paper 24839." National Bureau of Economic Research. https://www.nber.org/papers/w24839.pdf.

Walker, Joshua. 2019. *On Legal AI*. Washington, DC: Full Court Press.

Walters, Ed. 2021. (CEO at Fastcase), in discussion with the author.

Webb, Amy. 2016. *The Signals Are Talking: Why Today's Fringe Is Tomorrow's Mainstream*. New York: PublicAffairs.

Webb, Amy. 2019. "How to Do Strategic Planning Like a Futurist." *Harvard Business Review*, July 30, 2019. https://hbr.org/2019/07/how-to-do-strategic-planning-like-a-futurist.

Bibliography

Administrative Office of the U.S. Courts. "Public Access to Court Electronic Records." PACER: Federal Court Records. Accessed November 23, 2020. https://pacer.uscourts. gov/.

Agrawal, Ajay, Joshua Gans, and Avi Goldfarb. *Prediction Machines: The Simple Economics of Artificial Intelligence*. Boston, Massachusetts: Harvard Business Review Press, 2018.

Aidinlis, Stergios, Hannah Smith, Abi Adams-Prassl, and Jeremias Adams-Prassl. "Building a Justice Data Infrastructure." Oxford, UK: University of Oxford, September2020. https:// www.law.ox.ac.uk/sites/files/oxlaw/ukri_justice_data_report_fv_0.pdf.

Alarie, Benjamin, Anthony Niblett, and Albert Yoon. "How Artificial Intelligence Will Affect the Practice of Law." SSRN Scholarly Paper. Rochester, NY: Social Science Research Network, November 7, 2017. https://doi.org/10.2139/ssrn.3066816.

Alexander, Charlotte S., and Khalifeh al Jadda. "Using Text Analytics to Predict Litigation Outcomes." In *Law as Data: Computation, Text, and the Future of Legal Analysis*, 275–311. The SFI Press Seminar Series. Santa Fe: The SFI Press, 2019.

Allen, Susie. "Why We Know So Little about Disparities within the Federal Court System — and How That's Finally Changing." Kellogg Insight, July 10, 2020. https:// insight.kellogg.northwestern.edu/article/public-court-records-federal-judges-timing-efficiency-fairness.

Angwin, Julia, Jeff Larson, Surya Mattu, Lauren Kirchner, and ProPublica. "Machine Bias." *ProPublica*, 2016. https://www.propublica.org/article/machine-bias-risk-assessm ents-in-criminal-sentencing.

Arredondo, Pablo. (Co-Founder and Chief Product Officer at Casetext), in conversation with the author, February 10, 2021.

Artificial Lawyer. "France Bans Judge Analytics, 5 Years in Prison for Rule Breakers." *Artificial Lawyer* (blog), June 4, 2019. https://www.artificiallawyer.com/2019/06/04/fra nce-bans-judge-analytics-5-years-in-prison-for-rule-breakers/.

Artificial Lawyer. "Singapore Gov Subsidises Costs of Law Firm Tech Adoption." *Artificial Lawyer* (blog), May 9, 2019. https://www.artificiallawyer.com/2019/05/09/singap ore-gov-subsidises-costs-of-law-firm-tech-adoption/.

Ash, Elliott. "*The Political Economy of Tax Laws in the U.S. States*," 2015. https://api. semanticscholar.org/CorpusID:9658318.

Ash, Elliott, and Daniel L. Chen. "Case Vectors: Spatial Representations of the Law Using Document Embeddings." In *Law as Data: Computation, Text, and the Future of Legal Analysis*, 313–337. The SFI Press Seminar Series. Santa Fe: The SFI Press. 2019.

Ashley, Kevin D. *Artificial Intelligence and Legal Analytics: New Tools for Law Practice in the Digital Age.* Cambridge: Cambridge University Press, 2017.

A.T. v. Globe24h.com, 2017FC 114 *(CanLII)*, [2017] 4 FCR 310 (Federal Court 2017).

Atkinson, Katie. "Explainability for AI and Law in the Wild." Presented at the JURIX 2020: 33rd International Conference on Legal Knowledge and Information Systems, Virtual, December 10, 2020.

Badawi, Adam B., and Giuseppe Dari-Mattiacci. "Reference Networks and Civil Codes." In *Law as Data: Computation, Text, and the Future of Legal Analysis*, 339–365. The SFI Press Seminar Series. Santa Fe: The SFI Press, 2019.

Badeva-Bright, Mariya. (Co-founder Laws.Africa and Project Director AfricanLII, University of Cape Town), in discussion with the author, January 29, 2021.

Bailey, Jane, and Jacquelyn Burkell. "Revisiting the Open Court Principle in an Era of Online Publication: Questioning Presumptive Public Access to Parties' and Witnesses' Personal Information." *Ottawa Law Review* 48, no. 1 (2017): 143–181.

Barton, Benjamin H. "Some Early Thoughts On Liability Standards For Online Providers of Legal Services." *Hofstra Law Review* 44 (2015): 25.

Baumol, William J., David de Ferranti, Monte Malach, Ariel Pablos-Méndez, Hilary Tabish, and Lilian Gomory Wu. *The Cost Disease: Why Computers Get Cheaper and Health Care Doesn't.* New Haven London: Yale University Press, 2013.

Beauchamp-Tremblay, Xavier, and Antoine Dusséaux. "Not Your Grandparents' Civil Law: Decisions Are Getting Longer. Why and What Does It Mean in France and Québec?" *Slaw* (blog), June 20, 2019. http://www.slaw.ca/2019/06/20/not-your-gra ndparents-civil-law-decisions-are-getting-longer-why-and-what-does-it-mean-in-france-and-quebec/.

Bjornerud, Marcia. *Timefulness: How Thinking Like a Geologist Can Help Save the World.* Princeton, NJ: Princeton University Press, 2018.

Black, Ryan C., Ryan J. Owens, Justin Wedeking, and Patrick C. Wohlfarth. "The Influence of Public Sentiment on Supreme Court Opinion Clarity." *Law & Society Review* 50, no. 3 (2016): 703–732. https://doi.org/10.1111/lasr.12219.

Branting, Karl, Carlos Balhana, Craig Pfeifer, John Aberdeen, and Bradford Brown. "Judges Are from Mars, Pro Se Litigants Are from Venus: Predicting Decisions from Lay Text." In *Frontiers in Artificial Intelligence and Applications*, edited by Serena Villata, Jakub Harašta, and Petr Křemen, 215–218. IOS Press, 2020. https://doi.org/10. 3233/FAIA200867.

Broussard, Meredith. *Artificial Unintelligence: How Computers Misunderstand the World.* Reprint edition. The MIT Press, 2019.

Burkholder, Eric, Cole Walsh, and N. G. Holmes. "Examination of Quantitative Methods for Analyzing Data from Concept Inventories." *Physical Review Physics Education Research* 16, no. 1 (June 29, 2020): 010141. https://doi.org/10.1103/PhysRevPhysEducRes. 16.010141.

Byrom, Natalie. "Digital Justice: HMCTS Data Strategy and Delivering Access to Justice." The Legal Education Foundation, October2020. https://research.thelegaleduca tionfoundation.org/wp-content/uploads/2019/09/DigitalJusticeFINAL.pdf.

Bzdok, Danilo, Naomi Altman, and Martin Krzywinski. "Statistics Versus Machine Learning." *Nature Methods* 15, no. 4 (April2018): 233–234. https://doi.org/10.1038/nm eth.4642.

Cameron, Charles M., and Lewis A. Kornhauser. "What Courts Do ... And How to Model It." *SSRN Electronic Journal*, 2017. https://doi.org/10.2139/ssrn.2979391.

Canadian Lawyer. "Here's to Using Decision Trees in the New Year." 2014. https://www.canadianlawyermag.com/practice-areas/adr/here s-to-using-decision-trees-in-the-new-year/269264.

Carlson, Keith, Michael A. Livermore, and Daniel N. Rockmore. "The Problem of Data Bias in the Pool of Published U.S. Appellate Court Opinions." *Journal of Empirical Legal Studies* 17, no. 2 (2020): 224–261. https://doi.org/10.1111/jels.12253.

Carlson, Keith, Michael A. Livermore, and Daniel Rockmore. "A Quantitative Analysis of Writing Style on the U.S. Supreme Court." *Washington University Law Review* 93, no. 6 (January 1, 2016): 1461–1510.

Center, Berkman Klein. "Fairness and AI." *Medium*, April 20, 2020. https://medium.com/berkman-klein-center/fairness-and-ai-c5596faddd20.

Cervone, Luca, Monica Palmirani, and Fabio Vitali. "Akoma Ntoso." Akoma Ntoso Site. Accessed June 6, 2021. http://www.akomantoso.org/.

Chatila, Raja. "*Can AI Systems Be Trustworthy?*" Presented at the JURIX 2020: 33rd International Conference on Legal Knowledge and Information Systems, Virtual, December 11, 2020.

Chen, Daniel L. "Machine Learning and the Rule of Law." In *Law as Data: Computation, Text, and the Future of Legal Analysis*, 433–441. The SFI Press Seminar Series. Santa Fe: The SFI Press, 2019.

Clio. "2019 Legal Trends Report." Burnaby, Canada: Clio, 2019. https://www.clio.com/resources/legal-trends/2019-report/read-online/.

Colarusso, David. "Uncovering Big Bias with Big Data: An Introduction to Linear Regression." In *Data-Driven Law: Data Analytics and the New Legal Services*, edited by Edward Walters, 173–188. Boca Raton, FL: Auerbach Publications, 2018.

Complaints against Globe24h.com, 2015 CanLII 33260 (PCC) (Privacy Commissioner of Canada 2015).

Copus, Ryan, Ryan Hübert, and Hannah Laqueur. "Big Data, Machine Learning, and the Credibility Revolution in Empirical Legal Studies." In *Law as Data: Computation, Text, and the Future of Legal Analysis*, 21–57. The SFI Press Seminar Series. Santa Fe: The SFI Press, 2019.

Crews, Aaron. "The Big Move Toward Big Data in Employment." In *Data-Driven Law: Data Analytics and the New Legal Services*, edited by Edward Walters, 59–102. Boca Raton, FL: Auerbach Publications, 2018.

Data Protection Act 2018, Pub. L. No. c. 12, § Section 112.3 (2018). https://www.legislation.gov.uk/ukpga/2018/12/contents/enacted.

"Database." In Wikipedia, February 26, 2021. https://en.wikipedia.org/w/index.php?title=Database&oldid=1009139147.

Doctorow, Cory. "Data: The New Oil, or Potential for a Toxic Oil Spill?" Secure Futures by Kaspersky, 2020. https://www.kaspersky.com/blog/secure-futures-maga zine/data-new-toxic-waste/34184/.

Doctorow, Cory, Ken Liu, and Annalee Newitz. "Cory Doctorow - Tech in Sci-Fi & ATTACK SURFACE w/ Ken Liu & Annalee Newitz." Virtual, October 20, 2020. http s://www.youtube.com/watch?v=0LHCLd1FvLw.

Dumas, Marion, and Jens Frankenreiter. "Text as Observational Data." In *Law as Data: Computation, Text, and the Future of Legal Analysis*, 59–70. The SFI Press Seminar Series. Santa Fe: The SFI Press, 2019.

Eidelman, Vlad, Anastassia Kornilova, and Daniel Argyle. "Predicting Legislative Floor Action." In *Law as Data: Computation, Text, and the Future of Legal Analysis*, 117–150. The SFI Press Seminar Series. Santa Fe: The SFI Press, 2019.

Etzioni, Amitai, and Oren Etzioni. "Keeping AI Legal." SSRN Scholarly Paper. Rochester, NY: Social Science Research Network, February 2, 2016. https://doi.org/10.2139/ssrn.2726612.

European Commission. "Annexes to the Proposal for a Regulation of the European Parliament and of the Council Laying Down Harmonised Rules on Artificial Intelligence (Artificial Intelligence Act) and Amending Certain Union Legislative Acts." Brussels: European Commission, April 21, 2021.

European Commission. "Proposal for a Regulation of the European Parliament and of the Council Laying down Harmonised Rules on Artificial Intelligence (Artificial Intelligence Act) and Amending Certain Union Legislative Acts." Brussels: European Commission, April 21, 2021.

Ferro, Lisa, John Aberdeen, Karl Branting, Craig Pfeifer, Alexander Yeh, and Amartya Chakraborty. "Scalable Methods for Annotating Legal-Decision Corpora." In *Proceedings of the Natural Legal Language Processing Workshop 2019*, 12–20. Minneapolis, Minnesota: Association for Computational Linguistics, 2019. https://www.aclweb.org/anthology/W19-22.pdf.

Finley, Klint. "How Software Code Could Help You Grapple With the Legal Code." *Wired*, 2018. https://www.wired.com/story/how-software-code-help-grapple-with-legal-code/.

Fjeld, Jessica, Nele Achten, Hannah Hilligoss, Adam Nagy, and Madhulika Srikumar. "Principled Artificial Intelligence: Mapping Consensus in Ethical and Rights-Based Approaches to Principles for AI." *SSRN Electronic Journal*, 2020. https://doi.org/10.2139/ssrn.3518482.

Frankenreiter, Jens, and Michael A. Livermore. "*Computational Methods in Legal Analysis*." SSRN Scholarly Paper. Rochester, NY: Social Science Research Network, November 15, 2019. https://papers.ssrn.com/abstract=3568558.

Frey, Carl Benedikt. *The Technology Trap: Capital, Labor, and Power in the Age of Automation*. Princeton, NJ: Princeton University Press, 2019.

Frug, Sara. (Co-Director at Legal Information Institute), in conversation with the author, March 31, 2021.

Fry, Hannah. *Hello World: How Algorithms Will Define Our Future and Why We Should Learn to Live with It*. New York, NY: WW Norton, 2018.

Garg, Nikhil, Londa Schiebinger, DanJurafsky, and James Zou. "Word Embeddings Quantify 100 Years of Gender and Ethnic Stereotypes." *Proceedings of the National Academy of Sciences* 115, no. 16 (April 17, 2018): E3635–3644. https://doi.org/10.1073/pnas.1720347115.

Gates, Bill. *Road Ahead*. London: Viking USA, 1995.

Georgia et al. v. Public.Resource.Org, Inc., No. 18–1150 (Supreme Court of the United States April 27, 2020).

Glassmeyer, Sarah. "State Legal Information Census: An Analysis of Primary State Legal Information," 2014. http://www.sarahglassmeyer.com/StateLegalInformation/wp-content/uploads/2014/04/GlassmeyerStateLegalInformationCensusReport.pdf.

Gordon, Robert J. *The Rise and Fall of American Growth: The U.S. Standard of Living since the Civil War*. Princeton: Princeton University Press, 2016.

Grady, Kenneth A. "Mining Legal Data: Collecting and Analyzing 21st Century Gold." In *Data-Driven Law: Data Analytics and the New Legal Services*, edited by Edward Walters, 11–32. Boca Raton, FL: Auerbach Publications, 2018.

Grossman, Maura R., and Gordon V. Cormack. "Quantifying Success: Using Data Science to Measure the Accuracy of Technology-Assisted Review in Electronic Discovery." In *Data-Driven Law: Data Analytics and the New Legal Services*, edited by Edward Walters, 127–152. Boca Raton, FL: Auerbach Publications, 2018.

Hacker, Philipp. "A Legal Framework for AI Training Data." SSRN Scholarly Paper. Rochester, NY: Social Science Research Network, March 18, 2020. https://doi.org/10.2139/ssrn.3556598.

Hagendorff, Thilo. "The Ethics of AI Ethics: An Evaluation of Guidelines." *Minds and Machines* 30, no. 1 (March 1, 2020): 99–120. https://doi.org/10.1007/s11023-020-09517-8.

Hamilton, Isobel Asher. "Amazon Built AI to Hire People, but It Discriminated Against Women." *Business Insider*, October 10, 2018. https://www.businessinsider.com/amazon-built-ai-to-hire-people-discriminated-against-women-2018-10.

Hand, David J. *Dark Data: Why What You Don't Know Matters*. Princeton: Princeton University Press, 2020.

"Hansard." In Wikipedia. Wikipedia Foundation, November 27, 2020. https://en.wikipedia.org/w/index.php?title=Hansard&oldid=991040030.

Hao, Karen. 2020. "The Problems AI Has Today Go Back Centuries." *MIT Technology Review*, July 31, 2020. https://www.technologyreview.com/2020/07/31/1005824/decolonial-ai-for-everyone/.

Heaven, Will Douglas. "AI Is Wrestling with a Replication Crisis." *MIT Technology Review* (blog), November 12, 2020. https://www.technologyreview.com/2020/11/12/1011944/artificial-intelligence-replication-crisis-science-big-tech-google-deepmind-facebook-openai/.

Heaven, Will Douglas. "Predictive Policing Algorithms Are Racist. They Need to Be Dismantled." *MIT Technology Review*, July 17, 2020. https://www.technologyreview.com/2020/07/17/1005396/predictive-policing-algorithms-racist-dismantled-machine-learning-bias-criminal-justice/.

Hebbar, Prajakta. "CJI Bobde Says AI Won't Be Used For Decision-Making in Supreme Court." *Analytics India Magazine* (blog), December 16, 2019. https://analyticsindiamag.com/cji-bobde-says-ai-will-not-be-used-for-decision-making-in-supreme-court-but-for-case-management/.

Henderson, Bill. "Can Intrapreneurship Solve the Innovator's Dilemma? Law Firm Examples." In *Data-Driven Law: Data Analytics and the New Legal Services*, edited by Edward Walters, 199–210. Boca Raton, FL: Auerbach Publications, 2018.

Her Majesty's Courts & Tribunal Service. "Making the Most of HMCTS Data: HMCTS' Full Response and Update to Dr Byrom's Recommendations," October2020. https://assets.publishing.service.gov.uk/government/uploads/system/uploads/attachment_data/file/925341/HMCTS_Making_the_most_of_HMCTS_data_v2.pdf.

Hildebrandt, Mireille. "Law As Computation in the Era of Artificial Legal Intelligence. Speaking Law to the Power of Statistics." SSRN Scholarly Paper. Rochester, NY: Social Science Research Network, June 7, 2017. https://doi.org/10.2139/ssrn.2983045.

Hoadley, Daniel. (Head of Litigation Data at Mishcon de Reya LLP), in discussion with the author, June 2, 2021.

Hoadley, Daniel. "Open Access to Case Law–How Do We Get There?" *Internet Newsletter for Lawyers* (blog), November 23, 2018. https://www.infolaw.co.uk/newsletter/2018/11/open-access-case-law-get/.

Hodgins, Kristin. Director of Legal Operations, Government of British Columbia, Canada), in discussion with the author, February 19, 2021.

Holmes, Jr., Oliver Wendell. "The Path of the Law." *Harvard Law Review* 10 (1897): 457.

Illowsky, Barbara, and Susan Dea. "*Introductory Statistics*." OpenStax, updated 2020 2013. https://openstax.org/details/books/introductory-statistics.

Jayasuriya, Kumar. "Data Mining in the Law Firm: Using Internal Expertise to Drive Decision Making." In *Data-Driven Law: Data Analytics and the New Legal Services*, edited by Edward Walters, 189–198. Boca Raton, FL: Auerbach Publications, 2018.

Jockers, Matthew L. *Macroanalysis: Digital Methods and Literary History*. Champaign, IL: University of Illinois Press, 2013.

Kabiri, Nika, Ed Sarausad, and Rahul Dodhia. "Quantifying the Quality of Legal Services: Data Science Lessons." In *Data-Driven Law: Data Analytics and the New Legal Services*, edited by Edward Walters, 153–172. Boca Raton, FL: Auerbach Publications, 2018.

Katz, Daniel Martin, Michael J. Bommarito, II, and Josh Blackman. "A General Approach for Predicting the Behavior of the Supreme Court of the United States." *PLOS ONE* 12, no. 4 (April 12, 2017): e0174698. https://doi.org/10.1371/journal.pone.0174698.

Kelly, Richard. "Vellum: Printing Record Copies of Public Acts." Research Briefing. UK Parliament, August 15, 2018. https://commonslibrary.parliament.uk/research-briefings/cbp-7451/.

Kerner, Hannah. "Too Many AI Researchers Think Real-World Problems Are Not Relevant." *MIT Technology Review*, August 18, 2020. https://www.technologyreview.com/2020/08/18/1007196/ai-research-machine-learning-applications-problems-opinion/.

Klingenstein, Sara, Tim Hitchcock, and Simon DeDeo. "The Civilizing Process in London's Old Bailey." *Proceedings of the National Academy of Sciences* 111, no. 26 (July 1, 2014): 9419–9424. https://doi.org/10.1073/pnas.1405984111.

Knight, Will. "About 40% of Europe's 'AI Companies' Don't Use Any AI at All." *MIT Technology Review*, March 5, 2019. https://www.technologyreview.com/2019/03/05/65990/about-40-of-europes-ai-companies-dont-actually-use-any-ai-at-all/.

Knight, Will. "The Dark Secret at the Heart of AI." *MIT Technology Review*, April 11, 2017. https://www.technologyreview.com/2017/04/11/5113/the-dark-secret-at-the-heart-of-ai/.

Lefrak, Mikaela. "D.C. Bills In Limbo As Fences Block Hand-Delivery To Congress." *DCist* (blog), February 1, 2021. https://dcist.com/story/21/02/01/dc-laws-in-limbo-no-delivery-to-congress/.

Legal Services Corporation. "Simplifying Legal Help." LSC - Legal Services Corporation: America's Partner for Equal Justice. Accessed June 7, 2021. https://www.lsc.gov/node/3500.

Légifrance. "Article 33 - LOI N° 2019–222 Du 23 Mars 2019 de Programmation 2018–2022 et de Réforme Pour La Justice (1)." Légifrance, March 24, 2019. https://www.legifrance.gouv.fr/eli/loi/2019/3/23/JUST1806695L/jo/article_33.

Liptak, Adam. "Accused of 'Terrorism' for Putting Legal Materials Online (Published 2019)." *The New York Times*. May 13, 2019, sec. U.S. https://www.nytimes.com/2019/05/13/us/politics/georgia-official-code-copyright.html.

Lissner, Michael. (Executive Director at Free Law Project), in discussion with the author, February 22, 2021.

Livermore, Michael A, Vladimir Eidelman, and Brian Grom. "Computationally Assisted Regulatory Participation." *Notre Dame Law Review* 93 (2018): 977–1034.

Livermore, Michael A., and Daniel N. Rockmore. "Distant Reading the Law." In *Law as Data: Computation, Text, and the Future of Legal Analysis*, 3–19. The SFI Press Seminar Series. Santa Fe: The SFI Press, 2019.

Livermore, Michael A., and Daniel N. Rockmore. eds. *Law as Data: Computation, Text, and the Future of Legal Analysis*. Santa Fe: SFI Press, 2019.

Lohr, Steve. "A.I. Is Doing Legal Work. But It Won't Replace Lawyers, Yet." *The New York Times*, March 19, 2017, sec. Technology. https://www.nytimes.com/2017/03/19/technology/lawyers-artificial-intelligence.html.

Luca, Michael, and Max H. Bazerman. *The Power of Experiments: Decision Making in a Data-Driven World*. Cambridge, Massachusetts: The MIT Press, 2020.

Lynch, H. Fernandez, D. J. Greiner, and I. G. Cohen. "Overcoming Obstacles to Experiments in Legal Practice." *Science* 367, no. 6482 (March 6, 2020): 1078–1080. https://doi.org/10.1126/science.aay3005.

Martin, Kingsley. "Deconstructing Contracts: Analytics and Contract Standards." In *Data-Driven Law: Data Analytics and the New Legal Services*, edited by Edward Walters, 22–58. Boca Raton, FL: Auerbach Publications, 2018.

McGill, Jena, and Amy Salyzyn. "Judging by Numbers: How Will Judicial Analytics Impact the Justice System and Its Stakeholders?" *Dalhousie Law Journal* 44, no. 1 (2021): (Forthcoming).

McGinnis, John O., and Russell G. Pearce. "The Great Disruption: How Machine Intelligence Will Transform the Role of Lawyers in the Delivery of Legal Services." *Actual Problems of Economics and Law* 13, no. 2 (July 18, 2019). https://doi.org/10.21202/1993-047X.13.2019.2.1230-1250.

Medvedeva, Masha, Michel Vols, and Martijn Wieling. "Using Machine Learning to Predict Decisions of the European Court of Human Rights." *Artificial Intelligence and Law* 28, no. 2 (June 1, 2020): 237–266. https://doi.org/10.1007/s10506-019-09255-y.

Meyer, Michelle N., Patrick R. Heck, Geoffrey S. Holtzman, Stephen M. Anderson, William Cai, Duncan J. Watts, and Christopher F. Chabris. "Objecting to Experiments That Compare Two Unobjectionable Policies or Treatments." *Proceedings of the National Academy of Sciences* 116, no. 22 (May 28, 2019): 10723–10728. https://doi.org/10.1073/pnas.1820701116.

Mobray, Andrew, and Philip Chung. (Co-Director and Executive Director AustLII [Australasian Legal Information Institute]), in discussion with the author, February 17, 2021.

Morris, Jason. (Principal Research Engineer, Symbolic Artificial Intelligence for the Singapore Management University Centre for Computational Law), in discussion with the author, March 16, 2021.

Mueller-Freitag, Moritz. "10 Data Acquisition Strategies for Startups." *Medium*, May 31, 2016. https://medium.com/@muellerfreitag/10-data-acquisition-strategies-for-startups-47166580ee48.

Narayanan, Arvind. "How to Recognize AI Snake Oil." Princeton University Department of Computer Science. Accessed November 14, 2020. https://www.cs.princeton.edu/~arvindn/talks/MIT-STS-AI-snakeoil.pdf.

Nayyer, Kim. (Edward Cornell Law Librarian, Associate Dean for Library Services, and Professor of the Practice at Cornell University), in discussion with the author, February 26, 2021.

Neal, Jeff. "Transforming Law into a Science." *Harvard Law Today*, November 10, 2020. https://today.law.harvard.edu/transforming-law-into-a-science/.

Obermeyer, Ziad, Brian Powers, Christine Vogeli, and Sendhil Mullainathan. "Dissecting Racial Bias in an Algorithm Used to Manage the Health of Populations." *Science* 366, no. 6464 (October 25, 2019): 447–453. https://doi.org/10.1126/science.aax2342.

O'Neil, Cathy. *Weapons of Math Destruction: How Big Data Increases Inequality and Threatens Democracy*. Reprint edition. New York: Broadway Books, 2017.

Pah, Adam R., David L. Schwartz, Sarath Sanga, Zachary D. Clopton, Peter DiCola, Rachel Davis Mersey, Charlotte S. Alexander, Kristian J. Hammond, and Luís A. Nunes Amaral. "How to Build a More Open Justice System." *Science* 369, no. 6500 (July 10, 2020): 134–136. https://doi.org/10.1126/science.aba6914.

Palmirani, Monica, and Fabio Vitali. 2020. "OASIS LegalDocumentML (LegalDocML) TC." Oasis Open, https://www.oasis-open.org/committees/tc_home.php?wg_abbrev= legaldocml.

Pasquale, Frank. "Battle of the Experts: The Promise and Peril of Automating Knowledge Work." Presented at the 2021 Canadian Association of Law Libraries Virtual Conference, Virtual, June 2, 2021.

Pasquale, Frank. *New Laws of Robotics: Defending Human Expertise in the Age of AI*. Belknap Press: An Imprint of Harvard University Press, 2020. https://www.amazon.ca/ New-Laws-Robotics-Defending-Expertise/dp/0674975227.

Pasquale, Frank, and Glyn Cashwell. "Four Futures of Legal Automation." *UCLA Law Review*, June 9, 2015. https://www.uclalawreview.org/four-futures-legal-automation/.

Pechenick, Eitan Adam, Christopher M. Danforth, and Peter Sheridan Dodds. "Characterizing the Google Books Corpus: Strong Limits to Inferences of Socio-Cultural and Linguistic Evolution." *PLOS ONE* 10, no. 10 (October 7, 2015): e0137041. https:// doi.org/10.1371/journal.pone.0137041.

Pillay, Carina. (Project Director SAFLII [Southern African Legal Information Institute]), in discussion with the author, February 24, 2021.

ProPublica. "Bills – ProPublica Congress API." ProPublica Website. Accessed July 4, 2021. https://projects.propublica.org/api-docs/congress-api/bills/.

Quartararo, Mike. "Technology: Search Terms Are Dead. Or Are They? | Above the Law." Above the Law, 2019. https://abovethelaw.com/2019/11/technology-search-term s-are-dead-or-are-they/.

Ransbotham, Sam. "Reskilling Talent to Shrink Technology Gaps." *MIT Sloan Management Review*, August 19, 2020. https://sloanreview.mit.edu/article/reskilling-talent-to-shrink-technology-gaps/.

Regulation (EU) 2016/679 of the European Parliament and of the Council of 27 April 2016 on the protection of natural persons with regard to the processing of personal data and on the free movement of such data, and repealing Directive 95/46/EC, Pub. L. No. 2016/ 679, EUR-Lex - 02016R0679–20160504 (2016). http://data.europa.eu/eli/reg/2016/679/oj.

Remus, Dana, and Frank S. Levy. "Can Robots Be Lawyers? Computers, Lawyers, and the Practice of Law." SSRN Scholarly Paper. Rochester, NY: Social Science Research Network, November 27, 2016. https://doi.org/10.2139/ssrn.2701092.

Runciman, David. "Diary: AI." *London Review of Books*, January 25, 2018. https:// www.lrb.co.uk/the-paper/v40/n02/david-runciman/diary.

Salter, Shannon. (Chair at Civil Resolution Tribunal of British Columbia, and adjunct professor at the UBC Allard School of Law), in discussion with the author, February 18, 2021.

Schmitt, Carolyn, Jessica Fjeld, and Ryan Budish. "In Principle and In Practice | Berkman Klein Center," July 4, 2020. https://cyber.harvard.edu/story/2020-04/principle-and-pra ctice.

Secretariat, Treasury Board of Canada, and Treasury Board of Canada Secretariat. "Consolidated Federal Acts and Regulations in XML – Open Government Portal." Open Government Portal. Accessed July 4, 2021. https://open.canada.ca/data/en/data set/eb0dee21-9123-4d0d-b11d-0763fa1fb403.

Smith, Brad, Carol Ann Browne, and Bill Gates. *Tools and Weapons: The Promise and the Peril of the Digital Age.* New York: Penguin Press, 2019.

Soh, Jerrold. (Assistant Professor of Law and Deputy Director, Centre for Computational Law at the Singapore Management University), in discussion with the author, March 24, 2021.

Soh, Jerrold. "When Are Algorithms Biased? A Multi-Disciplinary Survey." SSRN Scholarly Paper. Rochester, NY: Social Science Research Network, April 20, 2020. https://doi.org/10.2139/ssrn.3602662.

Soh, Jerrold, How Khang Lim, and Ian Ernst Chai. "Legal Area Classification: A Comparative Study of Text Classifiers on Singapore Supreme Court Judgments." In *Proceedings of the Natural Legal Language Processing Workshop 2019*, 67–77. Minneapolis, Minnesota: Association for Computational Linguistics, 2019. https://doi.org/10.18653/v1/W19-2208.

Spiegelhalter, David. *The Art of Statistics: Learning from Data.* New York: Viking, 2019.

Statista Research Department. "Size of the Global Legal Services Market 2015–2023." Statista. Accessed March 21, 2021. https://www.statista.com/statistics/605125/size-of-the-global-legal-services-market/.

Strickson, Benjamin, and Beatriz De La Iglesia. "Legal Judgement Prediction for UK Courts." In *Proceedings of the 2020 The 3rd International Conference on Information Science and System*, 204–209. New York, NY, USA: Association for Computing Machinery, 2020. https://doi.org/10.1145/3388176.3388183.

Sutherland, Sarah. "Artificial Intelligence and Bias: Social Impacts of a Technical Solution." *Slaw* (blog), August 13, 2019. http://www.slaw.ca/2019/08/13/artificial-intelli gence-and-bias-social-impacts-of-a-technical-solution/.

Sutherland, Sarah. "Exploration of Attributes Associated with User Behaviour in Online Legal Research." *Canadian Law Library Review* 45, no. 2 (2020): 10–13.

Sutherland, Sarah. "Quantifying the Value of Legal Information." *Slaw* (blog), June 1, 2017. http://www.slaw.ca/2017/06/01/quantifying-the-value-of-legal-information/.

Sutherland, Sarah. "So There's Been Some Buzz about Legal Data Lately …." *Slaw* (blog), March 29, 2018. http://www.slaw.ca/2018/03/29/so-theres-been-some-buzz-a bout-legal-data-lately/.

Sutherland, Sarah. "Using Data to Leverage Access to Justice." *Slaw* (blog), August 1, 2013. http://www.slaw.ca/2013/08/01/using-data-to-leverage-access-to-justice/.

Taleb, Nassim Nicholas. *The Black Swan: The Impact of the Highly Improbable.* 2nd ed. New York: Random House, 2010.

Toit, Neil du. (AfricanLII Data Scientist, University of Cape Town), in conversation with the author, February 10, 2021.

Treasury Board of Canada Secretariat. "Consolidated Federal Acts and Regulations in XML." Open Government Portal, October 1, 2013. https://open.canada.ca/data/en/da taset/eb0dee21-9123-4d0d-b11d-0763fa1fb403.

Treasury Board of Canada Secretariat. "Open by Default and Modern, Easy to Use Formats." Government of Canada Website, June 27, 2019. http://open.canada.ca/en/content/open-default-and-modern-easy-use-formats.

Turek, Matt. "Explainable Artificial Intelligence." Defense Advanced Research Projects Agency. Accessed July 4, 2020. https://www.darpa.mil/program/Explainable-artificial-intelligence.

Underwood, Ted. *Distant Horizons: Digital Evidence and Literary Change*. Chicago: University of Chicago Press, 2019. https://www.amazon.ca/Distant-Horizons-Digital-Evidence-Literary/dp/022661283X/ref=tmm_pap_swatch_0?_encoding=UTF8&qid=&sr=.

University of Oxford Faculty of Law. "Unlocking the Potential of Artificial Intelligence for English Law," December 20, 2018. https://www.law.ox.ac.uk/unlocking-potential-artificial-intelligence-english-law.

Varian, Hal. "Artificial Intelligence, Economics, and Industrial Organization, Working Paper 24839." National Bureau of Economic Research, July2018. https://www.nber.org/papers/w24839.pdf.

Vivekanandan, V.C. (Vice Chancellor at Hidayatullah National Law University), in discussion with the author, February 24, 2021.

Wachter, Sandra, Brent Mittelstadt, and Chris Russell. "Why Fairness Cannot Be Automated: Bridging the Gap Between EU Non-Discrimination Law and AI." SSRN Scholarly Paper. Rochester, NY: Social Science Research Network, March 3, 2020. https://doi.org/10.2139/ssrn.3547922.

Wachter-Boettcher, Sara. *Technically Wrong: Why Digital Products Are Designed to Fail You*. New York, NY: WW Norton, 2017.

Wade, Michael, Amit Joshi, Mark J.Greeven, RobertHooijberg, and Shlomo Ben-Hur. "How Intelligent Is Your AI?" *MIT Sloan Management Review*, 2020. https://sloanreview.mit.edu/article/how-intelligent-is-your-ai/.

Walker, Joshua. 2019. *On Legal AI*. Washington, DC: Full Court Press

Wallach, Wendell. "Machine Morality: Bottom-up and Top-down Approaches for Modeling Human Moral Faculties," 2005, 9.

Wallach, Wendell, and Colin Allen. *Moral Machines: Teaching Robots Right From Wrong*. Oxford University Press, 2008.

Walters, Ed. (CEO at Fastcase), in discussion with the author, February 12, 2021.

Walters, Edward. "Introduction: Data Analytics for Law Firms: Using Data for Smarter Legal Services." In *Data-Driven Law: Data Analytics and the New Legal Services*, edited by Edward Walters, 1–10. Boca Raton, FL: Auerbach Publications, 2018.

Walters, Edward J. ed. *Data-Driven Law: Data Analytics and the New Legal Services*. Boca Raton, FL: Auerbach Publications, 2018.

Washington University Law. "The Supreme Court Database." Accessed August 2, 2020. http://scdb.wustl.edu/.

Webb, Amy. "*How Futurists Cope With Uncertainty*." Medium, March 11, 2020. https://medium.com/swlh/how-futurists-cope-with-uncertainty-a4fbdff4b8c6.

Webb, Amy. "How to Do Strategic Planning Like a Futurist." *Harvard Business Review*, July 30, 2019. https://hbr.org/2019/07/how-to-do-strategic-planning-like-a-futurist.

Webb, Amy. *The Signals Are Talking: Why Today's Fringe Is Tomorrow's Mainstream*. New York: PublicAffairs, 2016.

Wendel, W Bradley. "The Promise and Limitations of Artificial Intelligence in the Practice of Law." *Oklahoma Law Review* 72 (2019): 30.

Winterton, Jules. (Chief Executive Officer, British and Irish Legal Information Institute (BAILII)), in discussion with the author, June 8, 2021.

Wolfram, Stephen. "Computational Law, Symbolic Discourse, and the AI Constitution." In *Data-Driven Law: Data Analytics and the New Legal Services*, edited by Edward Walters, 103–126. Boca Raton, FL: Auerbach Publications, 2018.

Yolmo, Yeshey Rabzyor. "Why Do Only 4% Of Indian Lawyers Use AI, Even Though 95% Of The Courts Are Digitised?" *Analytics India Magazine*, 2019. https://analytic sindiamag.com/legal-tech/.

Index

academic research 5, 12, 14, 116–117, 123
access to justice xvi, 3, 78, 102, 117
actively and passively collected data 43–44
acts *see* statutes
Africa 14–15, 36
Akoma Ntoso 37
algorithms 81, 101, 103, 117, 122; machine learning 55–56, 69, 96; regulation of 74
ambiguity 45–46, 80–81, 86, 133
analogy 59
analytics 82–83, 88, 89, 103; case law and 23; sensitivity in 71–72, 105; website 28
anonymization 19–20, 24
API (application programming interface) 42–43
artificial intelligence 93–94; approaches to 44; definition of 84, 93–94, 104; error in 102; ethics of 102–104; forecasts of 93, 98, 132; history of 2, 69, 104, 120; issues with 88–89; legal applications of 93, 94, 99; limitations of 94–95, 99, 104; regulation of 114–115; types of 95–97
Australia 16, 110, 111
Austria 24, 111
automation 93, 94, 130

bag-of-words 58–59
bias 44, 56, 59–60, 74, 75, 102; in publication 85; sampling 82; sources of 101
billable hour 27, 30, 70, 99
business data 4, 26–28, 113, 116

Canada 13, 21, 36, 110, 114
case law 7–8, 8, 23–25, 65, 85–86, 115–116; access to 19–20, 24, 115; in civil law jurisdictions 87, 129; history of 115; privacy and 13–14, 111–112;

publication of 65, 85; social aspects of 24, 112; structure of 65, 79, 85–86
categorical data 38, 39
citation networks 50, 62, 73, 86–87
citations 36, 43, 62, 87
civil codes 9–10, 22, 62, 67, 87
client confidentiality 31, 116
close reading 50–51
coding languages 37, 45–46, 113
colonies 3, 15, 67
complexity 2, 72–73
consumer applications 6
correlation and causation 29–31, 70–71
costs xv, 24, 83
court decisions *see* case law
court filings *see* dockets
courts and tribunals 7–9, 23–24, 115; data 85; history 115; interpreting legislation 86; privacy and 111–112; proceedings xv; processes 5–6, 14, 26, 131; as sources of data 23, 79, technology 24; *see also* case law and dockets
crime data 21, 71, 101
culture 84, 117, 121, 126, 129; acceptance of technology and **123**, 126; of legal organizations 67, 96, 116

data: acquisition of 31, 51; availability of 8, 13–16, 19–20, 78, 110–113, 124–125; collection of xix, **23**, 27, 43–44; formats 34, 40–41, 51–52, **53**, 70–71; quality 2, 66, 122; strategy 30, 31, 35; structure 26, 84–88
data systems 129; risks in 74
databases 42, 45, 46
debates, parliamentary 9, 22, 115
decision trees 60–61, *61*
deep data 36, 55
dockets 8, 23, 25

For Product Safety Concerns and Information please contact our EU
representative GPSR@taylorandfrancis.com
Taylor & Francis Verlag GmbH, Kaufingerstraße 24, 80331 München, Germany

www.ingramcontent.com/pod-product-compliance
Ingram Content Group UK Ltd.
Pitfield, Milton Keynes, MK11 3LW, UK
UKHW021455080625
459435UK00012B/513